MUSIC THERAPY FOR HANDICAPPED CHILDREN

Volume I

Hearing Impaired
Visually Impaired
Deaf – Blind

Wanda B. Lathom
Charles T. Eagle, Jr.
Editors

MUSIC THERAPY FOR HANDICAPPED CHILDREN
*Vol. I: for the Hearing Impaired, Visually Impaired
            and Deaf – Blind*
Wanda B. Lathom & Charles T. Eagle, Jr., editors

PRINTED IN USA
ISBN: 0-918812-76-3

Library of Congress Catalog Card No: 84-72744
Printers: Rose Printing, Inc., Tallahassee, Florida
2nd printing: September, 1996

For further information and catalogs, contact:

MMB Music, Inc.
Contemporary Arts Building
3526 Washington Avenue
Saint Louis, MO 63103-1019

Phone: 314 531-9635, 800 543-3771 (USA/Canada)
Fax: 314 531-8384
E-mail: mmbmusic@mmbmusic.com
Web site: http://www.mmbmusic.com

CONTENTS

MONOGRAPH 1

MUSIC THERAPY FOR HEARING IMPAIRED CHILDREN, Jean L. Buechler

MONOGRAPH 2

MUSIC THERAPY FOR VISUALLY IMPAIRED CHILDREN, Peggy Codding

MONOGRAPH 3
MUSIC THERAPY FOR DEAF-BLIND CHILDREN, Sr. Lucille J. Cormier

ILLUSTRATIVE FIGURES

MONOGRAPH 1

MONOGRAPH 2

THE PROJECT MUSIC MONOGRAPH SERIES
Foreword

The monographs in this series were prepared to be used in a "Special Project: A National In-Service Training Model for Educational Personnel Providing Music Education/Therapy for Severely/Profoundly Handicapped Children." This grant (No. G007091336) was made to the National Association for Music Therapy, Inc. and was funded through the Office of Special Education, 1979-82. The workshop trainers were Registered Music Therapists (RMTs) who were selected to attend one of the two National In-Service Training Institutes in Music Therapy held in Denton, Texas in June, 1980 and 1981.

During the First Institute (1980) and the year following, during which in-service workshops were given, it became apparent that more detailed information was needed concerning music therapy for specific diagnostic categories listed under the general area of "Severely-Profoundly Handicapped Children." Although the Institute participants demonstrated expertise in the area(s) in which they were employed, they needed more information to use in in-service workshops for personnel who worked with children from other diagnostic categories. Thus, some of the participants were asked to write monographs to provide information on their area.

Before the Second Institute (1981), the first draft of each monograph was sent to Wanda Lathom, Project Director, and Charles Eagle, Training Coordinator. They provided editorial comments and asked external reviewers for further suggestions. These led to the second draft, which was presented to the Second Institute.

Participants for the Second Institute were selected to work in modular units: (1) a team leader who was the author of a monograph, (2) a music therapist who had carefully reviewed the music therapy literature of the area, (3) a clinician currently working in the area who could demonstrate clinical techniques, and (4) a clinician currently working in the area who could demonstrate assessment techniques. Each team member made a presentation to the entire Institute and each team carefully reviewed the monograph related to their area. Thus, the entire Institute evaluated each monograph and the contributions of members of the modular team. This peer review was of great value in preparation of the third draft of the monograph, which included suggestions and material submitted by the modular team of other colleagues who could contribute to the contents. These drafts then were submitted to the Project Director and Training Coordinator for editorial review, and individual conferences were held with each author during a grant meeting held in Denver (November, 1981) after the annual conference of the National Association for Music Therapy. The fourth, and final, revisions were submitted by the authors in January, 1982. Thus, each monograph represents extensive work by the primary author and considerable peer review and contributions from music therapists throughout the country.

Each of the monographs presents pertinent music therapy research of the designated area, although a complete report would have been beyond the scope of some of the monographs. However, each author assumed the responsibility to review an extensive body of literature relevant to the area.[1] Through case histories, examples of techniques, and discussion, each author has made the relevance of this literature evident.

The monographs were initially written to accompany the goals and objectives for in-service training, as stated in *A Manual to Conduct In-Service Training Workshops for Music Educators, Administrators, Parents, and Special Educators.*[2] However, it has become obvious that the monographs will be of use to practicing clinicians, colleagues in related treatment areas, and to students who plan to enter the profession of music therapy. In most areas, it is particularly apparent that additional research is needed. Many suggestions are offered by the authors for researchers who wish to pursue this endeavor.

The challenge for our continued scholarly growth, both while working as students and as practicing music therapists, was stated by E. Thayer Gaston (1964):[3]

> This striving for continued learning, probably by avid reading, after formal education, ought to be a primary activity in the continued growth of music therapists. The constant goal of becoming a scholar should be prominent in every training program. It is an ingredient of the educative process that needs day-by-day emphasis. It should not be left to chance. To leave it out is to insist that students shall not go beyond their teachers.

As music therapists continue to study, to conduct research, and to share information, both within the profession and with others who attend in-service training workshops, the continued growth of the profession and the subsequent improved service to handicapped children will not "be left to chance."

---

[1]This search was aided by two working drafts of *Music therapy for handicapped children: An annotated and indexed bibliography* by Charles Eagle, which was published as part of the grant project. Other publications emanating from the project were *Music therapy: A behavioral guide for the mentally retarded* by Clifford K. Madsen, *An assessment manual in music therapy* by Donald E. Michel and Michael Rohrbacher, and *The role of music therapy in the education of handicapped children and youth* by Wanda Lathom.

[2]Lathom, W. (Proj. Dir.). *A manual to conduct in-service training workshops in MUSIC THERAPY for music educators, administrators, parents, and special educators* (rev. ed.). Lawrence, KS: National Association for Music Therapy, 1981.

[3]Gaston, E. T. Developments in the training of music therapists. *Journal of Music Therapy,* 1964, *1*(4), 148-150.

THE PROJECT MUSIC MONOGRAPH SERIES
Authors and Editors

MUSIC THERAPY FOR HANDICAPPED CHILDREN:

DEAF—BLIND. **Sr. Lucille Cormier, RMT,** Department of Music, College Misericordia, Dallas, Pennsylvania.

EMOTIONALLY DISTURBED. **Darlene Watson Paul, RMT,** Conservatory of Music, University of Missouri at Kansas City.

HEARING IMPAIRED. **Jean Buechler, RMT,** Broward Exceptional Adult Education, Ft. Lauderdale, Florida.

MENTALLY RETARDED. **Sara A. Carter, RMT,** Sunland Center, Tallahassee, Florida.

MULTI-HANDICAPPED. **Sr. Mariam Pfeifer, RMT,** St Joseph's Center and Marywood College, Scranton, Pennsylvania.

ORTHOPEDICALLY HANDICAPPED. **Mary Toombs Rudenberg, RMT,** Moody School, University of Texas Medical Branch, Galveston.

OTHER HEALTH IMPAIRED. **Lenore M. Schwankovsky, RMT,** and **Peter T. Guthrie,** Department of Music, California State University at Long Beach.

SPEECH IMPAIRED. **Susan Gurvich Miller, RMT,** Department of Music Therapy, Southern Methodist University, Dallas, Texas.

VISUALLY IMPAIRED. **Peggy Codding, RMT,** Department of Music, University of Wisconsin at Eau Claire.

AN ANNOTATED AND INDEXED BIBLIOGRAPHY. **Charles T. Eagle, Jr., RMT,** Department of Music Therapy, Southern Methodist University, Dallas, Texas.

EDITORS: **Wanda B. Lathom, Ph.D., RMT,** Professor of Music Therapy, Conservatory of Music, University of Missouri at Kansas City.
Charles T. Eagle, Jr., Ph.D., RMT, LPC, Division of Music, Southern Methodist University, Dallas, Texas.

PREFACE

Less than two years ago (October, 1982), the 1st Edition of the Project MUSIC Monograph Series was published. This 10-part monograph set, entitled *Music Therapy for Handicapped Children*, was one of several outcomes of a three-year, federally funded grant in music therapy. Over 200 practicing music therapists contributed directly to these monographs. Each of the authors has extensive clinical and academic experience and is expert in working with the handicapped about which s/he writes. The authors have spoken from the heart, candidly describing their professional experiences.

In the monographs, you will find clinical descriptions of the handicapped person, *how* the person can be clinically assessed, and *how* the music therapist works with this person. The monographs also contain research reports and theoretical positions, and outlines of activities and case studies, as well as illustrations, glossaries, and extensive lists of references. Examples are presented of progress notes and IEPs/IHPs. Stated goals, objectives, and techniques are also included.

The response to the monographs has been beyond our expectations. Music therapy clinicians, teachers, and administrators have been enthusiastic in their support of this Project. Other professionals have also been supportive, such as special educators, music educators, arts therapists, and parents of handicapped children.

For the 2nd Edition, we decided to combine the monographs into four volumes. *Volume 1* contains the three monographs on music therapy for hearing impaired, visually impaired, and deaf-blind children; *Volume 2*, music therapy for emotionally disturbed, mentally retarded, and speech impaired children; *Volume 3*, music therapy for multi-handicapped, orthopedically handicapped, and other health impaired children; *Volume 4*, an annotated and indexed bibliography of publications pertaining to music therapy for handicapped children. In all the volumes, the contextual essence of the original, 1st Edition, has been retained. This 2nd Edition has been edited primarily for structural and typographical errors and in some instances, for organizational purposes to allow for more cohesion.

There are many very nice people who have made this 2nd Edition of the monographs a reality. In particular, we extend our grateful appreciation to Dr. Lindsey Merrill, Dean of the Conservatory of Music, Dr. Jack Stephenson, Chairman of the Department of Music Education/Therapy, and Professor George Petrie, all of the University of Missouri at Kansas City; to Dr. Eugene Bonelli, Dean of the Meadows School of the Arts, Dr. Charles Joseph, Chairman of the Division of Music, and Dr. Ann Redmond, Department of Music Therapy, all of Southern Methodist University in Dallas, Texas; and to our graduate assistants at our two universities.

There are six persons who have been especially important and supporting to us as we continued the Project. John and Helen Miniter worked diligently and successfully to fulfill the requests of those who wanted the 1st Edition of the monographs, which was published through the Institute for Therapeutics Research. Steve Meseraull, who printed the 1st Edition and now publishes the 2nd, has been a tower of support. Paul Ackerman has been there from the beginning. Ruth Lathom and Pat Eagle have been concerned, caring, and loving throughout our efforts.

To all these lovely folks, we can only offer our thanks. To the hundreds of significant others, we owe a great deal and wish to express our deep gratitude for your understanding, close attention, and personal commitment to this work.

Kansas City
Dallas

Wanda Lathom
Charles Eagle

August, 1984

MONOGRAPH 1

MUSIC THERAPY FOR
HEARING IMPAIRED CHILDREN

Jean L. Buechler

ACKNOWLEDGMENTS

A large portion of the first section of this monograph, "Understanding the Disability," is excerpted with permission from *Module 144, Hearing Problems,* produced through A System of Personnel Development (ASPD), The University of Iowa, Iowa City, Iowa.

Deep appreciation is expressed to Elizabeth Koppelmann, a trusted friend for criticism regarding the grammatical structure and general clarity of expression of the material contained in this monograph.

Many thanks are extended to participants in the Second National In-service Training Institute in Music Therapy, Denton, Texas, for their suggestions for revision of the second draft of this monograph, especially Richard Graham, Wanda Lathom, George Petrie, Nancy Fortney, Lalene Kay, Leo Muskatevc, Jackie Dimmick, and Mary Ellen Huber.

UNDERSTANDING THE DISABILITY

This section of the monograph is concerned with understanding the disability of hearing impairment from a physical perspective. Beside definitions and diagrams, information is provided on some general considerations when working with hearing impaired students in a school setting. Using this background information, therapeutic methods are constructed for presentation in a subsequent portion of this monograph.

Definitions

The generic term, *hearing impairment,* indicates a hearing disability which may range in severity from mild to profound. This term is used especially in education and usually denotes any child who is in need of special services because of hearing loss. These services may range from selected seating and speech and language therapy in a regular classroom to a program in a special self-contained classroom for severely and profoundly hearing impaired children. Hearing impairment includes the subsets of deaf, deafened, and hard-of-hearing.

A *deaf* person is one whose hearing disability is so severe that, with or without a hearing aid (or even the finest amplification system), the person cannot process language or understand speech using only the auditory system.

A *deafened* person is an individual who has suffered a severe hearing impairment after having acquired speech. Since this impairment occurs sometime after birth, it is often referred to as adventitious deafness.

A *hard-of-hearing* person is one who has some degree of hearing loss but who, with or without the use of a hearing aid, has sufficient hearing to understand speech and to process language through audition or the hearing mechanism.

Dimensions of Hearing Ability

There are several dimensions of hearing ability which may be impaired. *Sensitivity* is the ability to hear soft or low intensity sounds. *Frequency range* is the dimension of low to high sounds, as on a musical scale, which can be measured precisely. The sound is perceived as pitch. *Intensity* is the dimension designated in decibels. The human perceives intensity as loudness. Other dimensions of hearing can be tested, but sensitivity, intensity, and frequency range of hearing are the most basic and most often tested when a hearing problem is suspected in a school-age child.

Threshold of Hearing

A person's *threshold of hearing* is that point at which a person can hear the softest sound of a given frequency in 50% of a given number of trials. Threshold of hearing is often referred to as hearing level. Hearing level, or threshold, is usually stated in decibels (dB), which is a relative measure of power or intensity. On hearing tests, 0 dB is the standard point for each frequency at which people with normal hearing begin to detect sounds. A person with a level of -10 dB would be able to detect a fainter sound than a person with a level of +10 dB. Normal hearing levels range from about -10 to +15 dB.

Pure Tone Audiometer

Schools usually have access to a hearing testing device which tests both frequency and intensity. This device is called a *pure tone audiometer.* There are many different types of audiometers, but the pure tone audiometer typically covers a frequency range from 125 cycles per second (or hertz) to 800 hertz (Hz). This range covers the most important frequencies for hearing and understanding speech, the critical range being between 500 and 2,000 Hz.

Audiometers have earphones for delivering sounds to the individual being tested. The person giving the test sets the various controls for pure tones at frequencies ranging from very low to very high. The individual being tested indicates when the tone is heard. Testing a number of frequencies is required because a person's threshold for hearing may vary at different frequencies. In other words, it may take a much greater intensity, or loudness, to reach threshold of hearing at one frequency than at another.

Results of pure tone audiometric examination are usually recorded on an *audiogram*. An audiogram is reproduced in Figure 1. Notice that the audiogram is a graphic chart which depicts the hearing sensitivity (measured in frequency, or Hz) of the ear relative to a scale of normalcy (0 level). Intensity (measured in decibels, or dB) indicates how much louder than normal the sound must be to reach threshold.

FIGURE 1

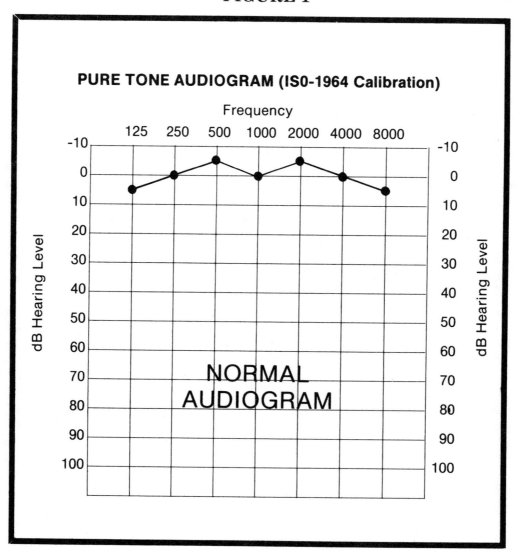

The Ear and Hearing

In the process of hearing, sound waves (vibrations of molecules in air or another medium) are collected by the outer ear and passed through the middle ear into the inner ear; there the sound is changed in the cochlea into nerve impulses. The nerve impulses travel through the eighth (auditory) nerve, are transmitted to several brain levels, and are perceived at the cortex. (See Figure 2.) Hearing may be impaired because of problems at any point in the chain described above. Sometimes psychological problems can result in a loss of functional hearing.

FIGURE 2

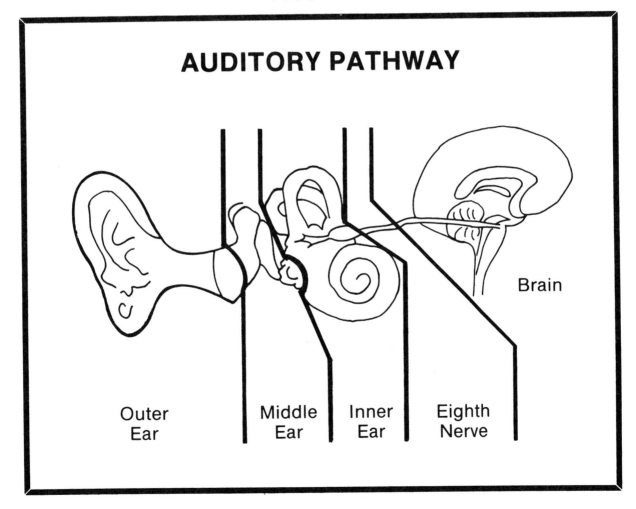

FIGURE 3

Classification of Hearing Losses

PERIPHERAL LOSSES

Conductive Losses

PROBLEMS IN OUTER AND/OR MIDDLE EAR

Sensorineural Losses

PROBLEMS IN RECEPTION IN THE INNER EAR OR
TRANSMISSION IN THE EIGHTH NERVE

CENTRAL LOSSES

Usually in brain
pathways or cortex.

FIGURE 4

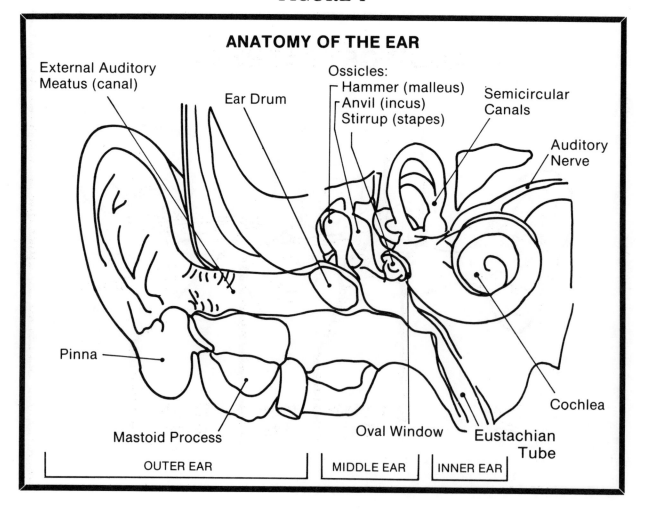

ANATOMY OF THE EAR

Hearing losses can be classified by location. *Conductive losses* are caused by problems in the sound traveling up to the inner ear from the outer ear. A *sensorineural loss* may result from damage to the cochlea of the inner ear or the auditory nerve to the brain. When both conductive and sensorineural losses are present, the result is called a *mix loss*. *Central losses* are caused by poorly understood conditions of the brain. (See Figure 3.)

Conductive losses are never total. Even if there is no opening into the ear, sound can be made loud enough to set the bones of the head into vibration, and therefore, the vibrations can reach the cochlea in the inner ear. Most conductive losses are not this severe. Causes of conductive losses include wax in the ear canal, damage to the ear drum, and diseases of the middle ear.

The middle ear has three tiny bones, or ossicles, which permit the transmission of sound from the ear drum to the fluid of the inner ear. The middle ear cavity is filled with air, and the air pressure in the middle ear is equalized with the air pressure outside the body through the eustachian tube. The various parts of the ear are diagrammed in Figure 4.

Many conductive problems arise in the middle ear. The middle ear may develop growths, or it may become infected with germs entering through the eustachian tube. A common malady is excessive ear pressure in the middle ear if the eustachian tube does not open periodically to equalize pressure. The ossicles may stiffen, or the foot plate of the innermost ossicle (the stirrup) may become fixed in the oval window leading to the inner ear. Conductive problems may be transitory or persistent, i.e., acute or chronic. Fortunately, most of these conductive problems can be improved by medical or surgical treatment.

Referring again to Figure 1, one sees an essentially normal audiogram. The zero line is an average of the intensity needed to reach threshold at each frequency for normal ears. The fluctuation shown above and below the zero line is within the normal range. You would expect some such variation in a test for normal children. However, Figure 5 represents a mild to moderate conductive hearing loss. Notice that the shape of the profile is essentially flat with the same variation expected in any audiogram. There is a slightly greater loss in the lowest frequencies. The loss is about 30 decibels; conductive losses could be greater or less than this level.

The two audiograms pictured in Figures 1 and 5 are *air conduction* audiograms. Air conduction means that the sound was delivered to the ears by earphones and traveled down the auditory canal by air. *Bone conduction* audiometric tests are administered by a vibrator which sets the bone of the skull into vibration. The sound bypasses the external auditory canal and is delivered directly to the end organ in the cochlea. Theoretically, bone conduction is a way to test the intactness of the sense organ. In a purely conductive loss (interference with the transmission of sound through the outer ear and middle ear to the inner ear), the air conduction thresholds would be poor but the bone conduction thresholds would be normal.

Sensorineural losses involve the end organ of hearing, or the eighth nerve to the brain. These losses may be total if the nerve is cut or if the cochlea is destroyed by disease or excessively loud noise. The losses may be congenital, as a result of inheritance or prenatal disease. Sensorineural losses may involve severe hearing loss at specific frequencies while other frequencies are essentially normal. Sensorineural losses are usually permanent and are not often helped by medicine or surgery. Because there is damage to the receptors of sound, rather than the conductors (outer and middle ears), sensorineural hearing losses may lead to significant problems in hearing and discriminating speech.

Central losses are the result of damage or malfunction in the brain or central nervous system. This type of loss may produce difficulty in understanding or processing speech, even when hearing sensitivity is normal. Children with severe problems of this kind rarely are found in regular classrooms. They have difficulty learning speech and require

FIGURE 5

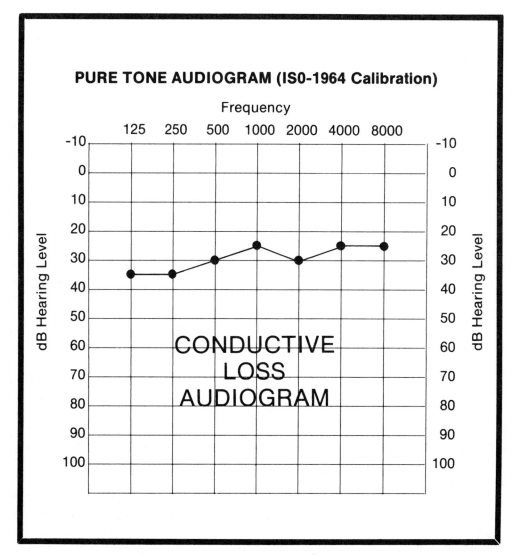

careful diagnosis to prevent their being mislabeled retarded or deaf. Children with mild central problems will most often be found in regular classrooms, but their problems are also difficult to diagnose.

Educational/Therapeutic Treatments

To plan therapeutic procedures, we must distinguish between deaf and hard-of-hearing. The deaf are most seriously handicapped in language. The most fundamental human task is learning language and speech. The language difficulty to a deaf child so limits the child's educational program that the child often must enroll in a school or in special classes for the deaf. Teaching the deaf is a highly specialized task. The regular classroom teacher usually will not have a deaf child in class. However, since the passage of PL 94-142, the tendency is toward the primary and intermediate age deaf student remaining in his/her home community with enrollment in a special self-contained class in a regular elementary school. It is not unlikely, therefore, to find these students participating in art, music, and physical education classes with pupils with normal hearing.

CONSIDERATIONS FOR MUSIC THERAPY

Further aspects of hearing impairment that must be considered in planning therapy/ education are addressed in this section. Emphasis is on the profoundly deaf student most often encountered by the music therapist in a school setting, especially in a school supported by an institution.

Many deaf students are difficult to assess for several reasons. First, no previous training/schooling may have been made available to the student due to lack of nearby programs and/or lack of financial aid to the family. Second, previous training may have taken place through improper placement in a large institution, as in the case of deaf persons who have been labeled retarded and placed in mental retardation facilities. Third, accurate historical information on the student's medical, psychological, and educational backgrounds is often difficult to obtain; this may be due to the promulgation of misinformation received during an initial misplacement or to the student. In some cases, the psychological and emotional strain on the family of the deaf student may result in the family's denial of additional related factors or in its desire to keep the student at his present level, rather than adjust to a growing, changing person.

For whatever reason, it is often the case that the deaf student is behind the average student academically. If previously misdiagnosed and placed in an institution for the mentally retarded, he will be much below the average student academically and socially, and probably have a seriously damaged self-concept as well.

Of course, there are also deaf students who are retarded, those whose dual disability was probably caused by a common type of brain damage. Other disabilities often found in combination with deafness are blindness and cerebral palsy. Since other monographs in this series have been written on the use of music therapy with the deaf-blind, the orthopedically handicapped, and the mentally retarded, this monograph will concentrate on the use of music therapy with students with hearing impairment, apart from other combined disabilities. However, some degree of delayed intellectual functioning will be taken into account, considering previously mentioned factors.

Music therapy programs with these students should stress the use and training of residual hearing and tactile reception of sound. Visual stimuli are paired with auditory and tactile stimuli for the most effective results. In the following section, the successes of variation of this integrated approach are described.

1. Is the aid being worn? The speech or hearing clinician should be able to inform the therapist when the aid should or should not be worn.
2. Is it operating? If not, check to be certain that the instrument is turned on and that the batteries are not dead. Instructions for doing this can be obtained from the speech and hearing specialist.
3. Is it removed for play or recess? Check to see that it has been replaced afterward so the child is ready for therapy.
4. Is it "whistling?" If so, the ear mold is probably loose and should be replaced.

The therapist may communicate with the hearing impaired child through reading and writing, assuming that the child can use these channels to supplement verbal communications. These children often depend on lipreading, or, as it is now called, speechreading. Speechreading means understanding speech by watching the speaker's lips, body language, and facial expression. We all speechread to some extent in difficult listening situations. Teaching to speechread involves helping the child to use many visual clues to gain meaning. The child must observe expressions, gestures, and situational clues.

Teaching lipreading is a job for a special teacher or clinician. Therapists/teachers can help by making it easier for the child to see them clearly and observing the following rules:

1. Do not stand in front of a strong light, such as a window.
2. Do not exaggerate your lip movement.
3. Do not change topics abruptly; help the child make the transition, perhaps with a few key words on the blackboard.
4. Have the child sit close to you if possible.
5. Face the child when giving instructions and information.
6. Speak slowly and clearly.

As previously mentioned, while the above communication channels may be applicable to many hearing impaired students, the music therapist is more likely to encounter those students who are deaf and/or multihandicapped. For these students, other avenues of communication need to be explored. Music is an ideal medium in these situations. In the following sections, suggestions are offered for working with profoundly handicapped, hearing impaired students.

RELATED LITERATURE ON THE USE OF MUSIC

In reviewing literature on the use of music with hearing impaired students, it is noted that the majority of reported studies deals with the student of normal intelligence, rather than the deaf, multihandicapped student, who is more frequently the client of the music therapist. However, it is also interesting to note that the literature, usually related to music education, does emphasize a therapeutic use of music: Music is used as a tool, a means to another end, rather than being an end in itself.

The literature emphasizes musical experiences involving rhythm, communication, and performance. Rhythmic activities have been used with the deaf to prepare the student for developing lipreading or clear speech. These activities require visual attending and imitation of gross motor patterns (Birkenshaw, 1965). Singing rhythms as well as movement activities and tactile discrimination of pitches have aided deaf students of normal intelligence in improving speech abilities (Fahey & Birkenshaw, 1972). Aiming toward total communication and expression of feelings, eurhythmics programs have been used in several schools for the deaf, instilling rhythmic concepts through whole-body movement in response to audio/tactile stimuli (Swaiko, 1974).

Hummell (1971) noted that Guberina's controversial "verbotonal method" of teaching speech to the deaf employed the creation of speech structures based on nursery rhymes and rhythms of body movements. In an interview with Fellendorf (1969), Guberina admitted that 20 to 30 minutes daily was needed to achieve good individual progress using this method. At first, syllables and groups of syllables were taught through selected gross patterns of body movement which he called "macromatricity." Later, nursery rhymes were used to develop acoustic memory. Guberina's method required special equipment which transformed the normal frequencies of the teacher/therapist's voice to lower, easier-to-perceive frequencies of the deaf student, which could be received with the aid of a headset.

It is recognized that the majority of persons who acquire deafness lose the ability to hear high frequencies first. Often, if the student has any residual hearing, low frequencies can be heard at varying decibels. In teaching music to deaf, multihandicapped children of normal intelligence, May (1961) stimulated their residual hearing using the fortissimo playing of notes in the low register of the piano. In a study by Madsen and Mears (1965), a low pitch of 50 Hz at both 60 decibels (dB) and 100 dB was found to desensitize the skin and raise the tactile threshold of three deaf subjects. If this can be generalized to a majority of deaf persons, there should be great potential in working with lower pitches, since both residual hearing and tactile threshold could be stimulated simultaneously. Using a similar method, May (1961) encouraged the use of each student's tactile sense. Students were taught to distinguish sounds of orchestral instruments by touching them while they were being played. Also, they participated in a rhythm band using instruments that afforded direct tactile stimulation through contact with the player's hands. Likewise, the tactile sense was responsible for a deaf trumpet student's ability to adjust his embouchure to produce the correct pitch at any given valve combination (Folts, 1977). The student learned this by placing his hand first on the bell of the teacher's trumpet as the correct pitch was played, and then placing his hand on the bell of his own trumpet, matching the vibrations, and thus producing a pitch of the same vibrations.

Tactile stimulation probably made the difference in a study by Korduba (1975). While testing third-grade achievers unable to hear sound under 85 dB above the threshold of normal hearing, it was found that deaf students performed duplication of the number of beats per measure apart from actual rhythmic impulse arrangement, better than normal hearing students tested in the same manner. It is very possible that the vibrations coming from the drums provided additional tactile cues to those students who, because of their deafness, had become more receptive to tactile stumuli. Thomas (1976) reported using a combination of tactile stimulation and visual cues in establishing a program for 10 deaf, retarded adults. This integral technique aided in developing activities designed to increase attending skills, improve motor coordination, and provide socialization skills.

In the endeavor to provide performance and experiences in creativity for the deaf, tactile stimuli are utilized in other instances. In a Florida public school instrumental program, mainstreamed hearing impaired students participated in beginning and intermediate bands by learning to play instruments which offer vibratory feedback through the teeth (reed instruments) and the jawbone (violin and viola). The music program is an integral part of a total communications approach for these students ("Deaf People Can Hear Music?" 1980).

Reed instruments had been used earlier with older deaf students, but when a less complicated instrument was needed for young deaf children, Van Uden (1963) developed his own. This instrument was composed of a headset attached to an amplifier which fed the wearer sound, produced when the child simultaneously depressed keys on a small keyboard while blowing air through a special mouthpiece and tube, thereby creating a bellows effect. The instrument, which was produced and used in Europe, was also a good aid to stimulation of residual hearing and auditory training. Because vibrations could be felt through the player's lips, mouth, and teeth, the kazoo has been a useful instrument for deaf students, enabling them to grasp the concepts of high and low, loud and soft, and fast and slow. It has also been used to teach the deaf to read rhythms, eventually leading to improved verbal communication (Birkenshaw, 1975).

In summary, the literature on the uses of music with the hearing impaired emphasizes the value of aural and tactile stimulation within various musical activities. These would be useful approaches with deaf students of any level of intelligence. More literature describing the use of music with multihandicapped deaf persons would be helpful, however, and a welcome addition to the field of music therapy.

ASSESSMENT FOR MUSIC THERAPY

In assessing a hearing impaired student, it is helpful if the music therapist is familiar with fingerspelling and some manual signs, as well as the signs specifically needed to give directions during the assessment. (Sources are provided in a later section of this monograph for those who wish to obtain fingerspelling and sign language instruction.)

An occasional student will be able to lipread. There are, however, a large percentage of deaf students who are not familiar with lipreading, fingerspelling, or signs, but instead have developed their own mode of expressive communication, manual and oral. The music therapist may be able to locate other school professionals who are able to interpret for these students but more commonly, the therapist is on his own, since usually only those living with the deaf person are able to comprehend his unique expressive language. The therapist also must learn to deal with frustration which manifests itself frequently with deaf in the area of expressive language. The therapist must be patient and, through a variety of activities combined with an authentic expression of concern, allow the student to reduce such frustration, while still attempting to understand his messages.

The first item to be assessed should be degree of hearing impairment as related to musical sounds. The therapist needs to have available a cassette player or a phonograph with a detached speaker, a headset which will adapt either to the cassette player or phonograph, a large amplifier, and smaller rhythm instruments with a variety of pitches. A piano is also helpful. The therapist should present the deaf student with a paper-and-pencil activity such as tracing, copying, or drawing, placing the student with his back to the therapist. Individual instruments are then played close to each ear with the therapist recording any head movement in the direction of any given sound. When a profound degree of retardation is present, the therapist must also watch the student's eye movement in the direction of the sound or blinking eye movement in response to sounds. It is often found that a student has residual hearing for the lower pitched instruments only.

Secondly, the music therapist should test for musical sounds in combination. Recordings which emphasize bass tone are best since the high pitches are usually the first to be lost when deafness occurs. The student is instructed to play an instrument when music is heard and is also asked at various intervals if he is hearing the music. Recorded music is started and stopped at various intervals. If the student does not indicate, beyond question, that he hears the recording, the same procedure is followed using a headset.

There are three important items to remember about the use of a headset: (1) the music therapist must always show the student what is about to happen by placing the headset on himself, (2) the therapist must always remove a hearing aid before placing a headset on a student, and (3) the volume control must be at its loudest before placing the headset and starting the recording. If the student indicates the presence of some hearing, the therapist may try lowering the volume gradually to determine a comfortable level. However, if the student still gives no indication of hearing, the therapist should proceed with assessing the tactile response to sound.

In this portion of the assessment, the student is exposed to the vibrations produced by musical recordings through a large speaker or amplifier. It is necessary for certain portions of the student's body to come into direct contact with the sound vibration. This is done by placing the student's hands, feet, or rib cage against the speaker and noting reaction, either positive (smiling, vocalizing, getting closer, playing an instrument) or negative (pulling away quickly, crying). Again, as with the headset, the music therapist should show the student what is about to happen by demonstrating on himself first. The music selected for this activity should emphasize strong bass tones and a percussive, steady beat.

If a piano is available, another method of detecting residual/tactile hearing preference for high or low pitches is to have the student stand with his head near one end of the open piano case while the music therapist strikes chords or tone clusters loudly at the same end. The same exercise is repeated at the opposite end of the piano, with student reactions compared.

When the above assessment portions have been completed, the music therapist proceeds to evaluate the student in the same areas as students of varying exceptionalities: communication, academic, motor, emotional, and social skills. The only differences are that the therapist will be communicating directions via singing, lipreading, tactile stimulation, or some other method found helpful in the earlier stages of the assessment.

PLANNING A MUSIC THERAPY PROGRAM

When the assessment has been completed, the music therapist will prepare an evaluation report (see Appendix A) for the treatment team or diagnostic and evaluation team charged with preparing the Individualized Education Plan (IEP) or treatment plan for the student. Based on recommendations of the team, the music therapy goal will be formulated and documented on the Music Therapy IEP (see Appendix B). This is usually attached to the student's school IEP. However in some school districts the information may be transferred directly to the school IEP form (see Appendix C).

During therapy, the therapist measures the student's progress through the use of a Data Sheet (see Appendix D) containing objectives which may be easily and quickly recorded (see Appendix E), though some schools within institutions may require a separate Music Therapy Progress Report (see Appendix F). When therapy has been completed, the treatment team decides if new goals may be met through the use of music therapy. If it is determined that music therapy is no longer recommended, then this may be stated on the Music Therapy IEP, or a separate Termination of Service Report may be required (see Appendix G).

Music therapy must be provided, under PL 94-142, for any student for whom this service has been written on his IEP. Parents, teachers, therapists (including the RMT), and administrators may recommend that music therapy be included as a related service.

FUNCTIONING THROUGH MUSIC THERAPY

The music therapist has a responsibility as a member of the team of professionals working with the deaf student to initiate actions which will result in the student developing to his maximum potential. This may involve referring the student to other professionals, such as the audiologist, the speech clinician, the psychologist, or to a nearby medical facility. Any suspicions concerning the student's welfare should be checked with other knowledgeable professionals, including the classroom teacher and guidance counselor, and pursued through appropriate channels. The guidance counselor or social worker usually will make necessary contacts with parents or guardians. Often, deaf students have never been evaluated for a hearing aid, the assumption being that it would not help, and the music therapist discovers that the student does have significant residual hearing when listening to music through a headset. The therapist should then request a complete audiological examination with possible fitting for an appliance.

Certain preparations should be made in the music therapy setting itself to accommodate the hearing impaired student. First of all, the highest quality sound system should be used and should include a microphone and headset. The larger Orff-type instruments which transmit large amounts of vibrations should be part of the music therapy equipment, such as metallophones, individual tone bars, rosewood xylophones, and tunable drums. Mirrors are of great aid in stimulating oral communication through singing. Many varied-textured materials, preferably musical, may be helpful in stimulating the tactile sense. The idea is to stimulate all of the available senses in order to compensate for the disabled sense of hearing. In addition, there should be seating available very close to the music source for the hearing impaired, especially in a group situation involving students of varying disabilities. Floor mats are also helpful in positioning the deaf student to accept vibrations from various music sources, as well as for relaxation activities.

Several musical devices and instruments helpful in working with deaf students have been developed by Musitronic of Owatonna, Minnesota. These include electric pianos with built-in speakers and headsets; video learning screens which are attached electronically to the keyboard system so that any sounds are transformed into visible, musical symbols; pick-ups which can transfer acoustic guitars into amplified guitars; and mic-headsets which enable the student to "hear" his own vocalizations. In addition, pentatonic musical instruments for the deaf have been designed by Grayson (1972); instructions for constructing same are available from the Cowichan Centre for Gestalt learning in Duncan, British Columbia.

Some of this equipment represents a sizable budget outlay and some therapists may find it necessary or expedient to work with more standard musical equipment. However, regardless of the equipment available, the therapist must make maximum use of personal creativity when working with hearing impaired students.

GOAL-ORIENTED ACTIVITIES IN MUSIC THERAPY

In this section of the monograph, a number of activities, which are by no means inclusive, have been compiled for use with hearing impaired students. The activities are ordered according to the goals for which each is selected and grouped according to categories adopted for music therapy assessment: communication, academic, motor, and social skills, as well as emotional growth. Each activity lists the goals and objectives for which it was designed, equipment and materials needed, and procedures and techniques to be used in carrying out the activity.

Activities have been selected which do not require the use of excessively expensive equipment, but instead can be accomplished by using instruments and equipment normally found in most school music programs. Additionally, manual signs helpful for expression of musical terms are presented in Appendix H. These activities have been used successfully with hearing impaired students; however, each therapist should strive to adapt music therapy activities to his/her own student's needs.

Activity #1—Tactile Discovery

Goal: Given guidance in individual music therapy, the student will respond to musical vibrations by independently playing a musical instrument rhythmically for two or more measures at least for six consecutive sessions.

Objectives: (1) The student will demonstrate an awareness of musical vibrations through his tactile sense by reacting either positively or negatively to the tactile stimulus twice per session for three consecutive sessions. (2) The student will manually locate the source of sound vibrations when presented with the tactile stimulus twice per session for three consecutive sessions.

Equipment and Materials Needed: A stereo speaker is placed beneath a metal or plastic-top table so that the sound speaker is facing upward, almost against the underside of the table top. The table top is dampened and spread with shaving cream (foam). The moist, slippery top adds another sensory stimulus—smell—and helps the hands to glide over the table. Recording used should emphasize a steady, rhythmic bass and should be played at high volume but without distortion. (The therapist's own hearing may be protected by wearing ear plugs.)

Procedure: The student is seated at the prepared table and introduced to the slippery surface. The music is played to introduce the tactile stimulus. For Objective #1, the student will either jump or draw back from the stimulus or smile and proceed in the direction of the stimulus. For Objective #2, the student will reach toward the area of most intense stimulus (directly over the speaker). In both cases, the therapist should alternate periods of musical stimulus with periods of silence.

Special Techniques: When introducing the student to the slippery table surface, the therapist should first demonstrate and then using physical assistance, gently guide the student's hands over the table. If the student exhibits a negative reaction to the sound stimulus, the therapist should indicate that there is no danger and encourage the student to continue to overcome his tactile defensiveness.

Activity #2—Tactile Extension

Goal: Given guidance in individual music therapy, the student will respond to musical vibrations by independently playing a musical instrument rhythmically for two or more measures at least for six consecutive sessions.

Objective: The student will demonstrate an awareness of musical vibrations through his tactile sense by playing an instrument only when vibrations are felt twice each session for at least three consecutive sessions.

Equipment and Materials Needed: A stereo speaker is placed on the floor in front of the student's seat with the sound speaker facing upward. A variety of rhythm instruments is placed on a table in front of the student. Preferred instruments include wood block and mallet, maraca, tambourine, and claves, because the sounds produced may be felt in the hands of the player. Recordings should emphasize a steady, rhythmic bass, and should be played at a high volume but without distortion. The stereo bass adjustment should be set at maximum level, while the treble adjustment should be at minimum level.

Procedure: Have the student remove his shoes and place his feet on the speaker, as if it were a footstool. With the music on, request that the student play a given instrument; this may be done in imitation of the therapist. (Note: The maraca is played against the hand.) When the music stops, request that the student stop playing the instrument. Repeat this procedure, rewarding correct responses, until the student is starting and stopping with the music, no longer needing to imitate the therapist.

Special Techniques: Positive reinforcement may be provided to deaf students in several ways, depending on understanding and acceptance by the student. If the student is not tactually defensive, a pat on the shoulder/hand and a smile work well. If he understands a few signs, the therapist may sign "good work" or the universally accepted sign for "O.K." It is helpful to the student to use these signs in any event, since he will probably be learning to use them in other settings. At the end of each session, it is suggested that the therapist tell the student in sign, "Thank you for coming to music therapy. You did good work today. Goodbye."

Activity #3—Rythmic Performance

Goal: Given guidance in individual music therapy, the student will respond to music vibrations by independently playing a musical instrument rhythmically for two or more measures at least for six consecutive sessions.

Objectives: (1) The student will play rhythmically for one measure twice each session for three consecutive sessions. (2) The student will play rhythmically for two or more measures twice each session for six consecutive sessions.

Equipment and Materials Needed: Refer to Activity #2.

Procedure: Have the student remove his shoes and place his feet on the speaker, as if it were a footstool. With the music on, request that the student play a given instrument "the same as the music." The therapist plays an instrument simultaneously and rhythmically with the student, giving visual cues, and asks the student to play "the same as me." After the student is imitating the rhythmic playing of the therapist, the therapist drops out for a few beats, requesting that the student continue playing. The therapist gradually lengthens the time he is not playing along with the student to two or more measures.

Special Techniques: If the student is unable to play rhythmically in imitation after several sessions, physical assistance may be needed to help the student comprehend playing "the same as the music." In addition, a recording with a more regular bass beat may be needed.

Activity #4—Vocal Stimulation

Goal: Given guidance in individual music therapy, the student will respond to tactile and visual stimuli by humming or vocalizing two or more notes in imitation of the therapist at least for six consecutive sessions.

Objectives: (1) The student will hum/vocalize one note in imitation of the therapist twice each session for three consecutive sessions. (2) The student will hum/vocalize two or more notes in imitation of the therapist twice each session for three consecutive sessions.

(3) The student will hum/vocalize two or more notes in imitation of the therapist twice each session at least for six consecutive sessions.

Equipment and Materials Needed: A small, lightweight stereo speaker is recommended. Recordings should emphasize bass, though they need not be particularly rhythmic. The stereo bass adjustment should be set at a medium level. Volume should be only loud enough for vibrations to be felt easily.

Procedure: Place the speaker against the chest (rib cage) of the student. With the music on, place the student's hands against his larynx and the other hand against the therapist's larynx. After the therapist begins vocalizing, he should instruct the student to "make the same sound" so that the student will be able to feel similar vibrations coming from his own larynx. The therapist should be prepared to be patient, but immediately reward any positive response.

Special Techniques: In the above procedure, some students are helped to respond vocally when the therapist gently rubs his fingers across the student's larynx to stimulate vibrating vocal cords. Some students respond better if the therapist's vocal stimulus consists of repeated music stimuli in one or both ears. Also, some respond faster if the therapist sings directly into the ear with the best hearing while still maintaining the tactile stimulus.

Activity #5—Vocal Imitation

Goal: Given guidance in individual music therapy, the student will demonstrate improved oral communication through correctly imitating three sung vowel sounds ("ah," "ee," "oo") in isolation and each vowel paired with beginning consonants (l, f, and b, p, or m) at least for six consecutive sessions.

Objectives: (1) The student will sing three vowel sounds ("ah," "ee," "oo") in imitation of the therapist twice each session for three consecutive sessions. (2) The student will sing three vowel-consonant combinations ("lah," "lee," "loo") in imitation of the therapist twice each session for three consecutive sessions. (3) The student will sing nine vowel-consonant combinations ("lah," "less," "loo," "bah," "bee," "boo," "fah," "fee," "foo") in imitation of the therapist twice each session for six consecutive sessions.

Equipment and Materials Needed: An acoustic guitar and mirror are needed. The student and therapist are seated, facing one another. The mirror is placed beside the therapist's chair, facing the student. In other words, the student should be able to see the therapist's mouth and the reflection of own mouth simultaneously, facilitating the student's ability to compare mouth shapes.

Procedure: Sitting opposite the student, the therapist places one of the student's hands on his own larynx and the other on the therapist's larynx. The student is instructed to watch the therapist's mouth and make the same shapes and sounds with his own mouth while the therapist accompanies on the guitar. If the student fails to imitate this procedure correctly, he should be encouraged to check the mirror for accuracy in matching mouth shapes. When this activity becomes tedious for the student, a good alternative is to allow the student to strum the guitar while watching and imitating the therapist's sounds. Frequent positive reinforcement also encourages the student's persistent attention.

Special Techniques: Exaggerated lip/tongue movements and facial expression (i.e., smiling widely on the "ee" sound) help to give clear direction as well as make this a fun activity for children and adolescents. Occasionally, physical assistance will be needed, such as the therapist manually positioning the student's mouth or holding the student's hand in front of his face to enable him to feel the expelled air at the beginning of the "f" sound.

Activity #6—Pitch Imitation

Goal: Given guidance in individual music therapy, the student will demonstrate improved oral communication by singing high and low pitches, generally following pitch direction of a melodic line at least for six consecutive sessions.

Objective: The student will sing isolated high and low pitches on a given syllable in imitation of the therapist twice each session for six consecutive sessions.

Equipment and Materials Needed: A cassette recorder with a headset is needed. Prior to the session, the therapist should record a series of high and low pitches using his own voice for some examples and the low register of the piano for other examples (not pitches above the C below middle C). During the first session, the therapist will determine which pitches are heard by the student and produce another tape using only the pitches within the student's hearing range. Cassette player volume should be at maximum level without distortion, using maximum bass tone.

Procedure: The therapist and student are seated facing one another, the student wearing the headset. Before the music is started, the student is instructed to match his voice on a given syllable to the sounds he will hear on the recording. The therapist will help by moving his hand in a horizontal plane higher or lower to match the corresponding taped pitches. (The therapist will probably be able to hear accurately the pitches through the outside of the headset.) As the music is started, the therapist lipsings to cue the student, while giving the manual cues.

Special Techniques: The distances between pitches should be exaggerated (intervals greater than an octave), so that in attempting to imitate high and low, the student will sing pitches at least a fifth apart. It is often helpful to guide the student's hand with the therapist's while giving manual cues. Always keep the range of manual cues within the direct visual plane of the student so that he is not tempted to force his head up and back, straining the sound, or down on his chest, smothering or choking the sound.

Activity #7—Pitch Movement

Goal: Given guidance in individual music therapy, the student will demonstrate improved oral communication by singing high and low pitches, generally following pitch directions of a melodic line at least for six consecutive sessions.

Objective: The student will sing high and low pitches imitating the general direction of a melodic line for two phrases each session for six consecutive sessions.

Equipment and Materials Needed: A record or cassette recording within the hearing range of the student is needed, along with the accompanying player and headset. Volume should be at maximum level without distortion, using maximum bass tone. (See discussion of hearing range in Activity #6.)

Procedure: Refer to Activity #6.

Special Techniques: If the student lipreads, the corresponding lyrics of the recording can be used, either by having the student lipread the therapist's singing or by having him memorize the lyrics and use the lipreading only as a cue to matching the lyrics to corresponding pitches. If the hearing range of the student encompasses the singing range of his own voice, it is possible to tape the student's responses and allow him to listen to the same, as a source of pride in accomplishment or incentive for improvement.

Activity #8—Identification of Letters, Numbers, or Colors

Goal: Given guidance in individual or small group music therapy, the student will demonstrate improved pre-academic skills by identifying seven letters of the alphabet (A-G) twice per session at least for six consecutive sessions.

Objectives: (1) The student will match seven letters of the alphabet (A-G) to their written symbols twice per session for six consecutive sessions. (The objective would be broken down into six smaller objectives.) (2) The student will identify seven letters of the alphabet (A-G), given the fingerspelling for each, twice per session for six consecutive sessions. (This objective would be broken down into six smaller objectives.)

Equipment and Materials Needed: Either individual resonator bells or an Orff-type soprano metallophone may be used because of their resonating qualities, creating vibrations which act as tactile stimuli. The bells or bars of the metallophone should be coded with letters of the musical alphabet. The resonator bells or metallophone and mallet are placed before the student on a table. A small music stand, either free-standing or table-top model, is a helpful item to the therapist for presenting cues but is not absolutely necessary. The therapist will also need flash cards individually displaying the letters A-G.

Procedure: Only the bells or bars containing the coded letters being worked on a given session are placed before the student. The therapist demonstrates to the student how to receive the tactile stimuli when producing sound: The resonator bell is held in the palm of the hand as it is being struck; one finger of the student is placed barely against the edge of a metallophone bar as it is being struck. With the student in position to receive the tactile stimulus, the therapist displays cue card of a given letter and asks the student to find the same and play it. (It is preferable that two bars or bells of each letter be available as choices.) After rewarding a correct response, the procedure should be repeated for the next letter. When the student seems sure of two or more letters, the procedure should be repeated with the bells or bars set before the student in mixed array. If the student is able to match seven letters in mixed array for six consecutive sessions, he is ready for the next step.

The identification procedure is similar to the matching procedure except that instead of using flash cards as cues, the therapist uses fingerspelling, giving a manual cue for each letter. At first, each manual cue will need to be paired with the corresponding flash card cue for easier student comprehension. The flash cards are then gradually faded out.

Special Techniques: When striking bells or bars with a mallet, most deaf students do not effect a single note but rather two or more notes on each cue. This may be due to a tendency toward perseverance, a need for more tactile stimulation, or simply an inability to "hear when to stop." The therapist may want to correct this tendency during this activity or wait until the student is playing melodies (see Activity #9). There are several methods which may be helpful in effecting such correction: (1) physically assist the student in striking each bar once, and have him repeat the same independently; (2) catch the mallet in mid air after one strike, preventing any additional striking, and have the student repeat the procedure, gradually fading out the catching; and (3) teach the fingerspelling symbol for (1), and cue this together with the letter desired for each response.

This same activity may be adapted for identification of colors and numbers.

Activity #9—Reading Left to Right

Goal: Given guidance in individual or small group music therapy, the student will demonstrate improved pre-academic skills by sequentially reading a melodic line of coded music, left to right, twice each session for six consecutive sessions.

Objectives: (1) The student will strike a given bell, bar, or key once and only once at each cue twice per session for three consecutive sessions. (2) The student will read and play a coded, five-note melodic line left to right following the therapist's pointer, twice per session for three consecutive sessions. (3) The student will read and play a coded, five-note melodic line left to right as he points to each note himself, twice per session for three consecutive sessions. (4) The student will read and play a coded, five-note melodic line left to right, independent of pointing, twice each session at least for six consecutive sessions.

Equipment and Materials Needed: An electronic keyboard with enclosed speaker is the ideal instrument for this activity. The keys should be coded with colors, letters, or numbers, corresponding to the coded melodic line to be read. If such an instrument is unavailable, the equipment listed under Activity #8 will suffice, but will not offer as much tactile/aural stimulation. In addition to the keyboard, the therapist will need to construct a coded melody on heavy cardboard. It is helpful to include measure lines as a guide to the student when reading independently. Appropriate rests should also be included, so that the end result is rhythmically correct. (Interpret the "rest" to the student as the manual sign for "wait.")

Procedure: With the student seated at the electronic keyboard with either one of his hands, knees, or feet in contact with the speaker, have him experiment with the instrument by depressing several individual keys and experience the tactile sensations produced by the speaker's vibrations. Full volume should be used. After this, instruct the student to play each note once as the therapist points to it. (This activity should not be undertaken until Activity #8 has been mastered. See notes under Activity #8's "Special Techniques" for teaching the student to play one note at a time.) When the student can effect single-note playing, request that he play the notes left to right, following his own pointing. When this has been mastered, the student is instructed to read and play the music without pointing to the written notation. This activity has many built-in rewards for the student and, as such, is an excellent activity for increasing self-esteem.

Special Techniques: Please refer to the discussion regarding notation and interpretation of rests under "Equipment and Materials Needed." In addition, in pointing out the use of the measure lines to the student while reading the notation sequentially, have the student read "as far as the next line" and repeat this process until all measures have been played.

If the student's feet are used to make contact with the tactile stimulus, shoes should first be removed.

If the student possesses some degree of residual hearing, he may receive reinforcing feedback through the use of a headset plugged into the electronic keyboard.

Activity #10—Socialization Through Music

Goal: Given guidance in group music therapy, the student will demonstrate increased appropriate socialization with peers through rhythmically playing a musical instrument as a member of an instrumental group at least for six consecutive sessions.

Objectives: (1) The student will attend to the group leader by watching him for directions through one song twice each session for three consecutive sessions. (2) The student will follow manual directions for starting and stopping the playing of a given instrument twice each session for three consecutive sessions. (3) The student will play an instrument rhythmically, following manual cues of the leader for one phrase of a song, twice each session for three consecutive sessions. (4) The student will play an instrument rhythmically, following manual cues of the leader for an entire song, twice each session for six consecutive sessions.

Equipment and Materials Needed: Preferred instruments are those which can provide tactile and/or aural stimulation to the student: electric guitar with amplifier, electric Autoharp, electronic keyboard large Orff-type resonating instruments, reed instruments, or large drums. If none of these can be obtained, instruments should be used which at least enable the student to tactilely experience the beat of the music: tambourine, maraca, wood block, or claves. Guitars may be pre-tuned to a given chord. Keyboard chords may be color-coded. This activity is designed so that the student need only be concerned with one chord or a single note. It may be followed by a more complicated activity (see "Special Techniques").

Procedure: The student is seated near the front of the group with his instrument. The entire group is instructed that the leader will use downstrokes for all manual directions to "play" and the deaf manual sign for "stop" as the signal to stop playing; a double "stop" will signal the end of a song. The deaf student is instructed to continue to watch the leader for directions. At the end of each song, strong positive reinforcement of the student's participation helps to maintain attention. Emphasis should be placed on the contributions of each member of the group. Then the performance via cassette tape may provide reinforcement for the entire group. A headset may allow the deaf student to hear some of the music.

Special Techniques: It is best to select songs which are rhythmically and melodically simple. Much eye contact with the deaf student is necessary to maintain Objective #1. Some physical assistance may be necessary until the student comprehends the idea of playing on each downbeat. If this activity is too simple for the student or if he has already accomplished these objectives, the therapist should offer him the opportunity for individual or small group instruction on one of the instruments until he has mastered a few notes or chords and is able to play music involving more than one harmonic change.

GLOSSARY

Audiology: The science of sound or hearing.

Audiometry: The measurement of the threshold for hearing tones relative to their intensity and frequency.

Aural: Received through the sense of hearing.

Bilateral: Pertaining to both sides of the body.

Decibel: A unit representing degree of loudness.

Extensity: An attribute of musical sound representing an association with the size of the sounding body; this attribute suggests that relatively low tones are used to secure volume.

Fingerspelling: A mode of communication employing the fingers of either hand in various configurations representing the letters of the American alphabet.

Frequency: Number of vibrations per second, often indicated by the sign or the abbreviation cps (cycles per second) or Hz (hertz); pitch.

Laryngology: The field of medicine concerning the larynx (voice box) and associated structures.

Manual English: A communications approach fusing fingerspelling, signs based on American Sign Language, and invented sign forms.

Otology: The field of medicine concerning the ears.

Presbycousis: A normal type of hearing loss which occurs with aging.

Reference tone: A pure tone of 1000 cps representing a fixed base from which loudness and intensity measurements are made.

Signed English: A communications approach using American Sign Language in which the message is encoded and expressed in accordance with the syntactical rules of the English language.

Sign language: A communications method employing arbitrarily formed signs (gestures) or sign phrases, not universally understood.

Tonal islands: Sensitive regions between the tonal lacunae.

Tonal lacunae: Isolated regions of frequency to which a person cannot respond.

Total communication: The simultaneous or progressive use of the full spectrum of language modes: gestures, sign language, speech, lipreading, fingerspelling, reading, and writing.

Unilateral: Pertaining to one side of the body.

REFERENCES

Birkenshaw, L. Teaching music to deaf children. *The Volta Review,* 1965, *65,* 352-358.

Birkenshaw, L. Consider the lowly kazoo. *The Volta Review,* 1975, *75,* 440-444.

Deaf people can hear music? *Florida Music Director,* 1980, *34*(2), 17.

Fahey, J. & Birkenshaw, L. Bypassing the ear: The perception of music by feeling and touch. *Music Educators Journal,* 1972, *58*(8), 44-49.

Fellendorf, G. The verbotonal method. *The Volta Review,* 1969, *71,* 213-224.

Folts, M. Deaf children cannot play a musical instrument...can they? *The Volta Review,* 1977, *77,* 453-456.

Grayson, J. A playground of musical sculpture. *Music Educators Journal,* 1972, *58*(8), 50-54.

Hummel, C. The value of music in teaching deaf students. *The Volta Review,* 1971, *73,* 224-228, 243-249.

Korduba, O. M. Duplicated rhythmic patterns between deaf and normal hearing children. *Journal of Music Therapy,* 1975, *12,* 136-146.

Madsen, C. & Mears, W. The effects of sound upon the tactile threshold of deaf subjects. *Journal of Music Therapy,* 1965, *2,* 64-68.

May, E. Music for deaf children. *Music Educators Journal,* 1961, *47*(3), 39-42.

Preferred signs for instructional purposes. Austin: Texas Educational Agency, 1978.

Swaiko, N. The role and value of an eurhythmics program in a curriculum for deaf children. *American Annals of the Deaf,* 1974, *119*(3), 321-324.

Thomas, M. W. Implications for music therapy as a treatment modality for the mentally ill deaf. *Voice of the Lakes* (Newsletter of the Great Lakes Region, National Association for Music Therapy), 1976, *76*(1), 19-22.

Van Uden, A. Instructing prelingually deaf children by the rhythms of bodily expression—Its possibilities and difficulties. *Proceedings of the International Congress on Education of the Deaf and of the 41st Meeting of the Convention of American Instructors of the Deaf. Washington, 1963.*

BIBLIOGRAPHY

Christopher, D. *Manual communication.* Baltimore: University Park Press, 1978.

Common medical terminology. Chicago: Abbott Laboratories, 1975.

Guralnik, D. (Ed.) *Webster's new world dictionary of the American language.* (Rev. ed.) New York: World Publishing, 1973.

Lundin, R. *An objective psychology of music* (2nd ed.). New York: Ronald Press, 1967.

Seashore, C. *Psychology of music.* New York: Dover Publications, 1967.

SELECTED READINGS AND RESOURCES

Additional handicapping conditions among hearing impaired students. Washington: Gallaudet College, 1973.

Alcorn, S. K. *Tadoma method of teaching speech to deaf children.* Talledega, AL: Southeast Regional Center for Deaf-Blind Children.

Arlington Developmental Center. *Sensory stimulation activities for early developmental levels.* Talladega, AL: Southeast Regional Center for Deaf-Blind Children, 1977.

Austin, G. *Bibliography on deafness.* Silver Spring, MD: National Association of the Deaf, 1976.

Bang, C. A world of sound and music. In *Claus Bang: A music therapy event.* Hicksville, NY: M. Hohner, 1977.

Bell, J. W. Seeing sound. *Scholastic Arts,* 1970, *70*(1), 26-29.

Birkenshaw, L. A suggested program for using music in teaching deaf children. *Proceedings of the International Conference on Oral Education of the Deaf, II,* Clarke and Lexington Schools for the Deaf, 1967.

Bladegroen, W. *The body image in relation to the physical education of pre-lingually deaf children.* Talladega, AL: Southeast Regional Center for Deaf-Blind Children, 1962.

Bolton, B. (Ed.). *Psychology of deafness for rehabilitation counselors.* Baltimore: University Park Press, 1976.

Burns, L. Music in deaf education. *Music Journal,* 1965, *23*(11).

California State Department of Education. *Audiology.* Sacramento, CA: Southwest Regional Center for Deaf-Blind Children, 1978.

Costello, P. Music for the deaf. *The Volta Review,* 1964, *66*(2).

Cull, J. & Hardy, R. *Educational and psychosocial aspects of deafness.* Springfield, IL: Charles C Thomas, 1974.

Dicarlo, L. M. Some relationships between frequency discrimination and speech reception performance. *Journal of Auditory Research,* 1962, *2*(1), 37-49.

Epley, C. In a soundless world of musical enjoyment. *Music Educators Journal,* 1972, *58*(8), 55.

Erber, N. F. Auditory visual perception of speech. *Journal of Speech and Hearing Disorders,* 1975, *40,* 481-492.

Ficociello, C. & Rudin, D. *Movin' and groovin': A program for the development of auditory-motor integration.* Dallas: South Central Regional Center for Deaf-Blind, 1975.

Frisina, R. *A bicentennial monograph on hearing impairment: Trends in the U.S.A.* (1st ed.). Washington, DC: The Alexander Graham Bell Association for the Deaf, Inc., 1976.

Further studies in achievement testing, hearing impaired students. Washington: Gallaudet College, 1973.

Gadling, D. & Pokorny, D. *You've got a song.* Silver Spring, MD: National Association of the Deaf, 1979.

Galloway, H. F. Jr. & Bean, M. F. The effects of action songs on the development of body-image and body-part identification in hearing-impaired preschool children. *Journal of Music Therapy,* 1974, *11*(3), 125-134.

Giovanni, S. Music as an aid in teaching the deaf. In E. H. Schneider (Ed.), *Music Therapy 1959: Ninth Book of Proceedings of the National Association for Music Therapy* (pp. 88-90). Lawrence, KS: National Association for Music Therapy, 1960.

Graham, R. M. (Ed.). *Music for the exceptional child.* Reston, VA: National Commission on Instruction, Music Educators National Conference, 1975.

Guberina, P. Verbotonal method and its application to the rehabilitation of the deaf. *Proceedings of the International Congress on Education of the Deaf and the 41st Meeting of the Convention of American Instructors of the Deaf.* Washington, DC, 1963.

Gunderson, R. W. *Audio transducers.* Talladega, AL: Southeast Regional Center for Deaf-Blind Children, 1971.

Hammer, E. K. *Child growth and development and the child who is deaf.* Talladega, AL: Southeast Regional Center for Deaf-Blind Children, 1975.

Hodges, D. A. Human hearing. In D. A. Hodges (Ed.), *Handbook of music psychology.* Lawrence, KS: National Association for Music Therapy, 1980.

Hogan, L. C. et al. A music program for young deaf children—A 'mod' approach. *The Volta Review,* 1968, *68,* 561-565.

Huffman, J. et al. *Sign language for everyone.* Northridge, CA: Joyce Motion Picture Company, 1975.

Huffman, J. et al. *Talk with me.* Northridge, CA: Joyce Motion Picture Company, 1975.

Karchmer, M. A. & Trybus, R. J. *Who are the deaf children in 'mainstream' programs?* Washington: Gallaudet College, 1977.

Kent, M. S. *Language growth and development of the deaf child.* Talladega, AL: Southeast Regional Center for Deaf-Blind Children, 1971.

Kirchner, S. *Play it by sign.* Northridge, CA: Joyce Motion Picture Company, 1974.

Kirchner, S. *Signs for all seasons.* Northridge, CA: Joyce Motion Picture Company, 1977.

Kleffner, F. R. Hearing losses, hearing aids, and children with language disorders. *Journal of Speech and Hearing Disorders,* 1973, *38*(2), 232-239.

Knapp, R. A. A choir for total communication. *Music Educators Journal,* 1980, *66*(6), 54-55.

Lafon, J. C. Various aspects of auditory discrimination and their occurrence in aphasics and deaf children. *Revue de Laryngologie, Otologie, Rhinologie,* 1968, *89,* 393-400.

Lane, H. S. Psychological aspects of rehabilitating the deaf through music. In E. G. Gilliland (Ed.), *Music Therapy 1952: Second Book of Proceedings of the National Association for Music Therapy* (pp. 169-172). Lawrence, KS: National Association for Music Therapy, 1953.

McDermott, E. F. Music and rhythms—From movement to lipreading and speech. *Volta Review,* 1971, *73*(4), 229-232.

Mills, M. M. Voice and rhythm in the primary grades of the New Jersey School for the Deaf. *American Annals of the Deaf,* 1942, *87*(9).

Northern, J. L. & Down, M. P. *Hearing in children.* Talladega, AL: Williams and Wilkins Company, Southeast Regional Center for Deaf-Blind Children, 1974.

Ochlocknee Children's Center. *Characteristics of the hearing impaired child* [Curriculum in use at Ochlocknee Children's Center, Ochlocknee, GA]. Talladega, AL: Southeast Regional Center for Deaf-Blind Children.

Omer, J. L. *Evaluating the audiogram.* Talladega, AL: Interstate Printers and Publishers, Southeast Regional Center for Deaf-Blind Children, 1976.

O'Rourke, T. *A basic course in manual communication.* Silver Spring, MD: National Association of the Deaf, 1970.

Pahz, J. & Pahz, C. *Robin sees a song.* Silver Spring, MD: National Association of the Deaf, 1977.

Pirtle, M. & Seaton, K. P. Use of music training to actuate conceptual growth in neurologically handicapped children. *Journal of Research in Music Education,* 1973, *21*(4), 292-301.

Robbins, C. & Robbins, C. *Music with the hearing impaired: A resource manual and curriculum guide.* St. Louis: Magnamusic-Baton, 1980.

Ross, E. D. et al. Musical hallucinations in deafness. *Journal of the American Medical Association,* 1975, *231*(6), 620-622.

Salkin, J. & Schoop, T. Dance program for the hearing-impaired child. In B. Morkovin (Ed.), *Through the barriers of deafness and isolation.* New York: Macmillan , 1960.

Sander, M. V. *Modern miracles.* San Diego: M. S. Paquin, 1979.

Schein, J. P. *Education and rehabilitation of deaf persons with other disabilities.* Talladega, AL: Southeast Regional Center for Deaf-Blind Children, 1973.

Schein, J. (Ed.). *Education and rehabilitation of deaf persons with other disabilities.* Silver Spring, MD: National Association of the Deaf, 1974.

Schein, J. & Naiman, D. (Eds.). *Use of group techniques with deaf persons.* Silver Spring, MD: National Association of the Deaf, 1971.

Schiff, W. et al. *Electronic communication with deaf and deaf-blind persons.* Talladega, AL: Southeast Regional Center for Deaf-Blind Children, 1973.

Schwetz, F. Tone and speech hearing in acoustic trauma. *Monatsschrift Fuer Ohrenheilkunde und Laryngo-Rhinologie,* 1969, *103,* 105-110.

Shroyer, E. H. & Tweedie, D. (Eds.). *Monograph II—Perspectives on the multihandicapped hearing impaired child.* Washington: Gallaudet College, 1979.

Spicknall, H. W. Music for deaf and hard-of-hearing children in public schools. In E. T. Gaston (Ed.), *Music in therapy.* New York: Macmillan, 1968.

Stern, V. They shall have music. *The Volta Review,* 1975, *75,* 495-500.

Studies in achievement testing, hearing impaired students. Washington: Gallaudet College, 1973.

Swink, D. F. *Therapists and therapies with deaf people: The need for specialized training, attitude exploration, and novel approaches.* Talladega, AL: Southeast Regional Center for Deaf-Blind Children, 1979.

Traughber, S. H. *Discrimination made on musical stimuli by children institutionalized for deafness.* Unpublished master's thesis, Murray State College, Murray, KY, 1957.

Tweedie, D. & Shroyer, E. (Eds.). *Monograph III—Hearing impaired mentally retarded children.* Washington: Gallaudet College, 1979.

Van Dijk, J. *Multiply handicapped deaf children.* Talladega, AL: Southeast Regional Center for Deaf-Blind Children, 1970.

Vernon, McC. *Rubella and deafness.* Silver Spring, MD: National Association of the Deaf, 1968.

Vernon, McC. *Multiply handicapped deaf children.* Washington: Council for Exceptional Children, 1969.

Vernon, McC. *Multiple handicaps and deafness.* Silver Spring, MD: National Association of the Deaf, 1970.

Vettese, J. Instrumental lessons for deaf children. *The Volta Review,* 1974, *76*(4), 219-222.

Whitehurst, M. W. *Auditory training for children.* Washington, DC: Alexander Graham Bell Association for the Deaf, 1974.

Wisher, P. R. Creative dance for the deaf. *Music Journal,* 1965, *23*(11).

SELECTED FILMS

Auditory Assessment, 16mm sound/color film, 26 min; Title #154601; from the European Series: International Education of the Hearing Impaired Child. Rent or purchase from National Audiovisual Center, General Services Administration, Washington, DC 20409.

Cognitive Development, 16 mm sound/color film, 15 min; Title #000324; from the American Series: International Education of the Hearing Impaired Child. Purchase from National Audiovisual Center, General Services Administration, Washington, DC 20409.

Communicating Ideas Through Language (Part I). Order through Educational Media Distribution Center, 5034 Wisconsin Avenue, N.W., Washington, DC 20016.

Composed for You, 16mm sound/color film, 11.5 min. Purchase from National Association of the Deaf, 814 Thayer Avenue, Silver Spring, MD 20910.

The Deaf-Blind Child, 16 mm sound/color film, 23 min; Title #260410; from the European Series: International Education of the Hearing Impaired Child. Rent or purchase from National Audiovisual Center, General Services Administration, Washington, DC 20409.

The Developing Audio-Vocal System, 16mm sound/color film, 38 min; Title #268512; from the European Series: International Education of the Hearing Impaired Child. Rent or purchase from National Audiovisual Center, General Services Administration, Washington, DC 20409.

Developing Auditory Response Patterns, 16mm sound/color film, 44 min; Title #270211; from the European Series: International Education of the Hearing Impaired Child. Rent or purchase from National Audiovisual Center, General Services Administration, Washington, DC 20409.

Diagnostic Techniques, 16mm sound/color film, 8 min; Title #000328; from the American Series: International Education of the Hearing Impaired Child. Purchase from National Audiovisual Center, General Services Administration, Washington, DC 20409.

Ears and Hearing, 16mm black and white film, 10 min. Rent or purchase through Encyclopedia Britannica Films, Inc., 202 East 44th Street, New York, NY 10017.

Educational Diagnosis, 16mm sound/color film, 29 min; Title #000331; from the American Series: International Education of the Hearing Impaired Child. Rent or purchase from National Audiovisual Center, General Services Administration, Washington, DC 20409.

Learning to Speak, Part I, 16mm sound/color film, 20 min; Title #003711; from the American Series: International Education of the Hearing Impaired Child. Purchase from National Audiovisual Center, General Services Administration, Washington, DC 20409.

Learning to Speak, Part II, 16mm sound/color film, 25 min; Title #000168; from the American Series: International Education of the Hearing Impaired Child. Rent or purchase from National Audiovisual Center, General Services Administration, Washington, DC 20409.

Lisa Pay Attention, 16mm sound/color film, 22 min. Rent from Indiana University Audio-Visual Center, Bloomington, IN 47401.

Listen, 16mm sound/color film, 30 min; Title #004661; from the Western Maryland College Series. Purchase with or without captions from National Audiovisual Center, General Services Administration, Washington, DC 20409.

Montessori—A Core Curriculum for Hearing Impaired Children with Learning Disabilities, 16mm sound/color film, 21 min; Title #000344; from the American Series: International Education of the Hearing Impaired Child. Rent or purchase from National Audiovisual Center, General Services Administration, Washington, DC 20409.

A Preschool Lesson in Cued Speech, 16mm sound/color film, 7 min; Title #000350; from the American Series: International Education of the Hearing Impaired Child. Rent or purchase from National Audiovisual Center, General Services Administration, Washington, DC 20409.

Say It with Hands, a series of 26, 16mm black and white films, each a 30-minute lesson in manual communication; Title #003424. Purchase from the National Audio-visual Center, General Services Administration, Washington, DC 20409.

Sound Discrimination of Hearing Impaired, 16mm sound/color film, 25 min; Title #003440; from the American Series: International Education of the Hearing Impaired Child. Purchase from National Audiovisual Center, General Services Administration, Washington, DC 20409.

The Sound Perception Method, 16mm sound/color film, 39 min; Title #699203; from the European Series: International Education of the Hearing Impaired Child. Rent or purchase from National Audiovisual Center, General Services Administration, Washington, DC 20409.

Total Communication, 16mm sound/color film, 15 min; Title #004662; from the Western Maryland College Series. Purchase with or without captions from National Audiovisual Center, General Services Administration, Washington, DC 20409.

We Tiptoed Around Whispering, 16mm sound/color film, 23 min; Title #004663; from the Western Maryland College Series. Purchase from National Audiovisual Center, General Services Administration, Washington, DC 20409.

SELECTED VIDEOTAPES

Claus Bang: A Music Therapy Event, 1/2 in. VHS or Betamax, 3/4 in. U-matic video cassette. Rent or purchase from M. Hohner, Inc., Andrews Road, Hicksville, NY 11802.

I Can't Hear, But I Can Sing, 1/2 in. or 3/4 in. videotape, black and white, 10 min. Rent or purchase from Media Department, New York Medical College, Mental Retardation Institute, Valhalla, NY 10595.

Sensory Stimulation #2: Beginning Communication, 20 min. Rent free from South Central Regional Center for Services to Deaf-Blind Children, 2930 Turtle Creek Plaza, Dallas, TX 75204.

Sensory Stimulation #4: Tactile, 20 min. Rent free from South Central Regional Center for Services to Deaf-Blind Children, 2930 Turtle Creek Plaza, Dallas, TX 75204.

Sensory Stimulation #5: Auditory, 20 min. Rent free from South Central Regional Center for Services to Deaf-Blind Children, 2930 Turtle Creek Plaza, Dallas, TX 75204.

SUPPORT ORGANIZATIONS

Alexander Graham Bell Association
for the Deaf
3417 Volta Place, N.W.
Washington, DC 20007

American Association for Music Therapy
66 Morris Avenue
Springfield, NJ 07081
Telephone (201) 379-1100

American Instructors of the Deaf
5034 Wisconsin Avenue, N.W.
Washington, DC 20016

American Speech-Language-Hearing
Association
10801 Rockville Pike
Rockville, MD 20852

Centers and Services for
Deaf-Blind Children
Office of Special Education
Donohoe Building
7th and D Streets, S.W.
Washington, DC 20202

Closer Look
Box 1492
Washington, DC 20013

Council for Exceptional Children
1920 Association Drive
Reston, VA 22091

Gallaudet College
Kendall Green
Washington, DC 20002

International Rehabilitation Film
Review Library
20 West 40th Street
New York, NY 10018

National Association of Hearing and
Speech Agencies
814 Thayer Avenue, Room 201
Silver Spring, MD 20910

National Association of the Deaf
814 Thayer Avenue
Silver Spring, MD 20910

National Association for Music
Therapy, Inc.
1133 Fifteenth Street, N.W.
Suite 1000
Washington, DC 20005
Telephone (202) 429-9440

National Audiovisual Center
General Services Administration
Washington, DC 20409

APPENDIX A
Evaluation Report

NAME__Jerry Sky_____   D.O.B. 1/3/65   DATE 10/15/80

Jean L. Buechler, RMT

EVALUATION	GOALS
Jerry was evaluated for music therapy on 10/2/80. The assessment tool used was "Music Therapy Evaluation: Level 3" modified for the hearing impaired.	It is recommended that Jerry receive a complete audiological examination with the hope of being fitted with a hearing aid as soon as possible.
Jerry is a 15-year-old male previously diagnosed as profoundly deaf and moderately retarded. He went willingly with the music therapist to the music room and was very cooperative throughout the evaluation, often smiling and expressing thankfulness through manual communication, a form of communication that he appears to use and comprehend very well.	It is recommended that Jerry receive music therapy on an individual basis, twice weekly, to improve verbal communication, working toward a "total communications" approach for this student.
Jerry exhibited excellent gross and fine motor skills. He also excelled in communication skills, both receptive and expressive, when manual signing or fingerspelling was used. Jerry did exhibit some frustration, however, in not being able to express himself verbally. He tried to verbalize often but was only able to produce unintelligible sounds. Still, he continued to attempt to pair vocalizations to signs.	
While Jerry's academic skills were lower than the average for his age, he appeared to possess adequate basic skills to enable him to continue to progress in the classroom. He functioned relative to a student with a mild degree of retardation.	
On observation of Jerry in the classroom, it was noted that he is very social; in fact, he often helps the teacher by assisting with lower level students. His initial meeting with the music therapist was friendly and characterized by both initiated and responsive interactions.	
Jerry was found to have much residual hearing for individual instruments, for recorded music when a headset was used, and for amplified music.	

APPENDIX B
Music Therapy IEP

INDIVIDUAL EDUCATIONAL PLAN
MUSIC THERAPY

lent ___Jerry Sky___   Date of Implementation ___11/1/80___

ter ___Royal Palm School___   Therapist ___Jean L. Buechler, RMT___

Objectives	Number of Sessions/Times	Service Provider	Estimated Time Frame From	To	Date of Completion	Comments
Given guidance in individual ic therapy, Jerry will demon-te improvement in verbal ex-ssion by vocalizing the vowel ids, ah, ee, and oo, in song with percent accuracy, twice each ion for at least six consecutive ions.	20 minutes, 2 times per week	J. Buechler	11/1/80	2/1/81		
Given guidance in individual ic therapy, Jerry will demon-te improvement in verbal ex-ssion by vocalizing the beginning sonant sounds, buh, luh, and fuh, ong with 100 percent accuracy, ce each session for at least six secutive sessions.			2/1/81	6/1/81		

APPENDIX C
Individual Educational Plan (IEP)

The School Board of Broward County, Florida
INDIVIDUAL EDUCATIONAL PLAN (Continued)

Student: _____ Jerry Sky _____ Case #: 138-031-6827 _____

ANNUAL GOALS

	Perceptual Motor		Behavior/Social and Emotional Skills
	Pre-Academics		Pre-Vocational
	Self Help Skills		Vocational
	Academic and Skill Instruction	X	Other - Communication

Annual Goal: Improve verbal expression by vocalizing sounds, ah, $\overline{ee}$, & $\overline{oo}$, in song, 100% accuracy, 2x per session, 6 consecutive sessions _____

Instructor: J. Buechler, RMT

Short Term Objectives:

PPP				Anticipated Date of Mastery	Date Mastered
Level	Page	1.	Vocalize "ah"	11/30/80	
PPP					
Level	Page	2.	Vocalize "ee"	12/30/80	
PPP					
Level	Page	3.	Vocalize "oo"	1/30/81	
PPP					
Level	Page	4.			

Methods: Vocal stimulation through tactile stimuli paired with aural stimuli; imitation through visual stimuli _____

Materials: Guitar, cassette tape recordings of low frequency sounds, headset, mirror _____

Comments: 20-minute sessions, twice weekly _____

Annual Goal: Improve verbal expression by vocalizing initial consonant sounds, buh, luh, & fuh, in song, 100% accuracy, 2x per session, 6 consecutive sessions _____

Instructor: J. Buechler, RMT

Short Term Objectives:

PPP				Anticipated Date of Mastery	Date Mastered
Level	Page	1.	Vocalize "buh"	3/15/81	
PPP					
Level	Page	2.	Vocalize "luh"	4/15/81	
PPP					
Level	Page	3.	Vocalize "fuh"	6/1/81	
PPP					
Level	Page	4.			

Methods: Same as above methods _____

Materials: Same as above materials _____

Comments: Same as above comments _____

34

APPENDIX D
Music Therapy Data Sheet

MUSIC THERAPY DATA SHEET

Client   Jerry Sky   Reinforcers signed & tactile praise;   Code: + = Step done correctly
                                                 self-achievement
trand   Vocal Music   Verbal Command   ---   - = Step not done correctly

Objectives	Dates	11/13/80	11/18/80	11/20/80	11/25/80	11/27/80	11/30/80	12/3/80	12/5/80	12/10/80	12/12/80
Vocalizes "ah" - 2x6		+	+	+	+	+	+	Accomplished 11/30/80			
Vocalizes "ee" - 2x6					-	+	-	+	+	+	
Vocalizes "oo" - 2x3								-	-	+	

35

APPENDIX E
Updated Music Therapy IEP

INDIVIDUAL EDUCATIONAL PLAN
MUSIC THERAPY

Student _____ Jerry Sky _____   Date of Implementation _____ 11/1/80 _____

Center _____ Royal Palm School _____   Therapist _____ Jean L. Buechler, RMT _____

Objectives	Number of Sessions/Times	Service Provider	Estimated Time Frame From	To	Date of Completion	Commen
Given guidance in individual music therapy, Jerry will demonstrate improvement in verbal expression by vocalizing the vowel sounds, ah, ee, and oo, in song with 100 percent accuracy, twice each session for at least six consecutive sessions.	20 minutes, 2 times per week	J. Buechler	11/1/80	2/1/81	1/15/81	Very recept hard worke 1/30/
Given guidance in individual music therapy, Jerry will demonstrate improvement in verbal expression by vocalizing the beginning consonant sounds, buh, luh, and fuh, in song with 100 percent accuracy, twice each session for at least six consecutive sessions.			2/1/81	6/1/81		

APPENDIX F
Music Therapy Progress Report

MUSIC THERAPY DEPARTMENT

SUMMARY OF MONTHLY PROGRESS

Student ___Jerry Sky_____   Month ___January, 1981____

School ___Royal Palm School____   Date of Report _2/1/81___

During this month, _____Jerry_____ accomplished the following objectives from the ____Vocal Music_____ Strand(s) toward completion of goals stated on his/her current IEP:

Given guidance in individual music therapy, Jerry will demonstrate improvement in verbal expression by vocalizing the vowel sounds, ah, ee, and oo, in song with 100 percent accuracy, twice each session for at least six consecutive sessions.

Additional Comments:

Jerry has been very receptive and a hard worker. The above skills will be maintained through inclusion in music therapy activities during the remainder of the school year.

Therapist _____
                    Jean L. Buechler, RMT

APPENDIX G
Termination of Service Report

MUSIC THERAPY DEPARTMENT

TERMINATION REPORT

Student   Jerry Sky   Treatment Period 11/80-6/83

School   Royal Palm School   Date of Report   6/15/83

Treatment for Jerry Sky is being terminated at the end of this school year since he will be attending a local workshop program in the future. His progress has been steady, characterized by enthusiasm and hard work. Attainment of a hearing aid during the 1981-82 school year helped to hasten progress and enabled the student to be placed in a vocal group composed of normal and hearing-impaired students. His participation in the group has been effected at his maximum level.

Jerry is now communicating with peers using combined manual and verbal skills. Music therapy treatment goals and methods have been coordinated with those of speech therapy for maximum benefit to this student. Jerry continues to want to improve his verbal abilities.

It is recommended that Jerry continue to receive music therapy and speech therapy as part of his workshop program. Records will be made available from this school system to professionals working with Jerry in the future.

Therapist_____
Jean L. Buechler, RMT

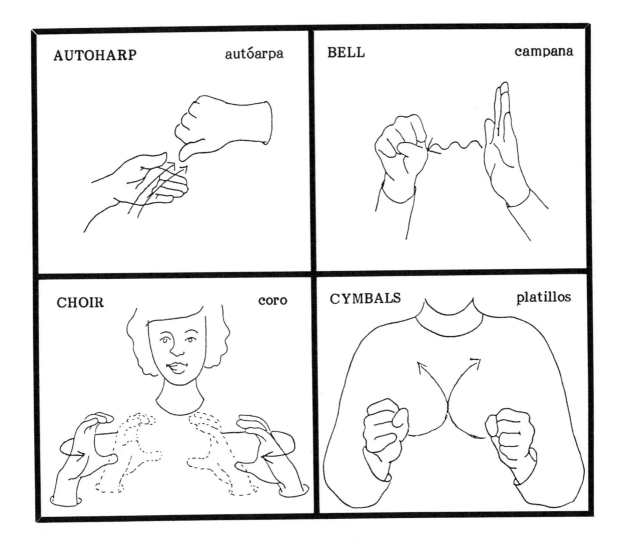

| AUTOHARP | autóarpa | BELL | campana |
| CHOIR | coro | CYMBALS | platillos |

*Adapted from *Preferred Signs for Instructional Purposes.* Austin, TX: Texas Education Agency, 1978.

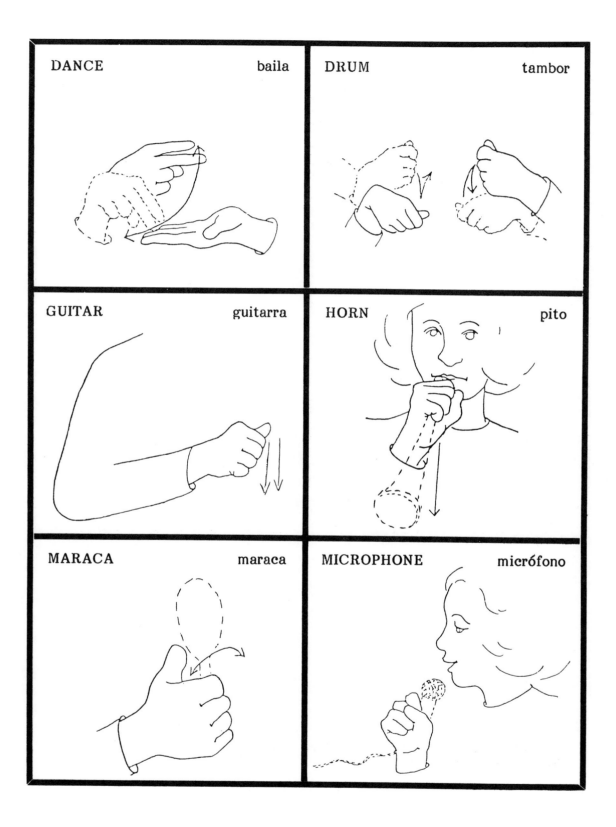

DANCE   baila   DRUM   tambor

GUITAR   guitarra   HORN   pito

MARACA   maraca   MICROPHONE   micrófono

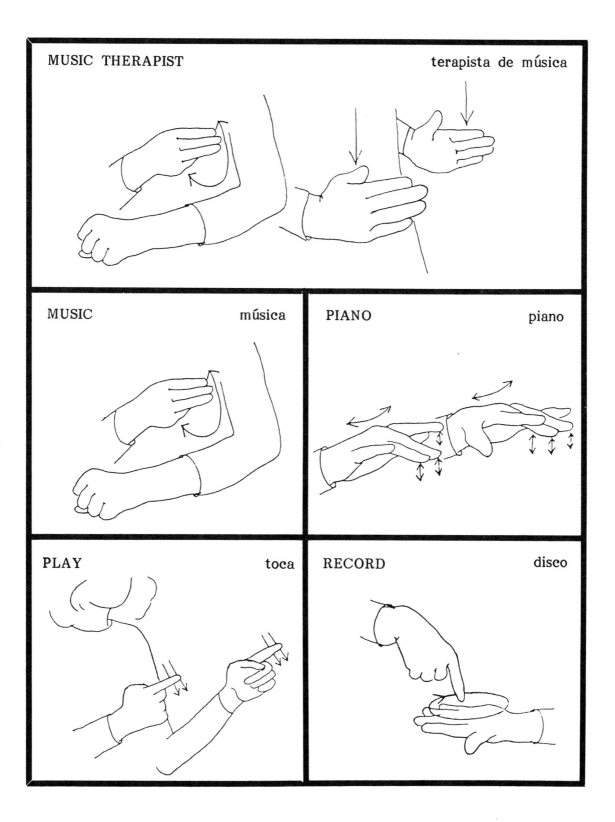

MUSIC THERAPIST   terapista de música

MUSIC   música   PIANO   piano

PLAY   toca   RECORD   disco

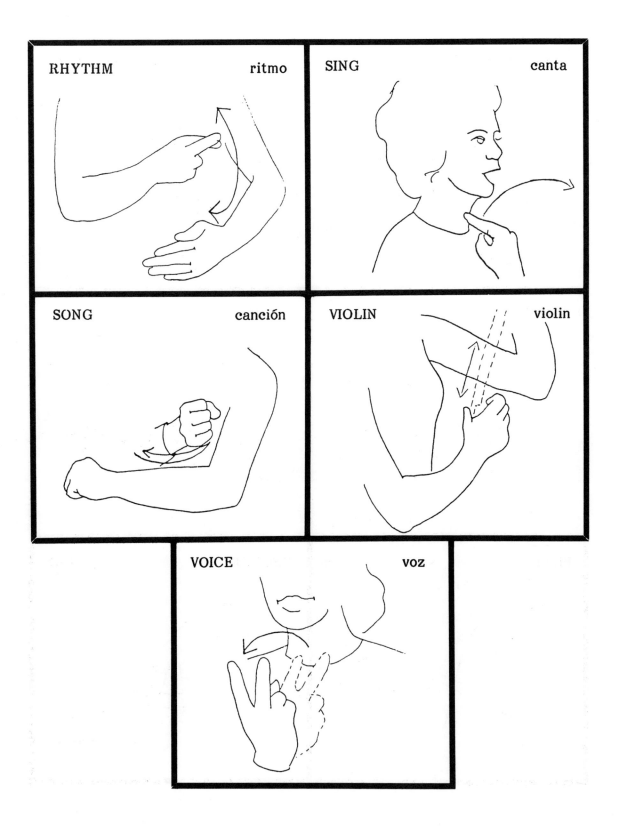

MONOGRAPH 2

MUSIC THERAPY FOR
VISUALLY IMPAIRED CHILDREN

Peggy Codding

ACKNOWLEDGMENTS

The author wishes to express her sincere appreciation to the following individuals for their contributions to this monograph:

To Dr. Wanda Lathom, RMT, and Dr. Charles Eagle, RMT, who gave so freely of themselves for so long, and without whose vision and concrete support, this monograph would not have been written.

To Doreen Veazie-Desmangles, RMT, who put her time and experience into the writing of a case study and program synopsis for inclusion in this monograph. Her contribution added so much to this effort. Her cooperation and generosity is deeply felt.

To Sr. Lucille J. Cormier, CND, RMT, who graciously offered herself as a resource, and her assessment tools for inclusion in this work.

To the staff of the Oak Hill School, Connecticut Institute for the Blind, who allowed me to include the case study and assessment tools in this monograph.

To the staff of the Tennessee School for the Blind who taught me to love teaching, gave me the opportunity to work with visually impaired children, and who allowed me to use material from the school curriculum guide in some sections of this monograph.

To Dr. Joseph L. Teeters—mathematician, artist, creative spirit—who designed and drew a diagram of the eye especially for this monograph.

To Dr. Blaine F. Peden and Dr. Robert Sampson who have taught me to write more effectively, and have served as my editors throughout this project.

To Ms. Karen Horning, future RMT, whose work as my student assistant at the University of Wisconsin-Eau Claire has enabled me to complete this and other projects.

DEDICATION

To
my friend, my teacher
Mary Nelle Council
and to
the children
at the Tennessee School for the Blind
in Donelson, Tennessee,
who taught me to see the world
through their senses
and their sensitivity.

INTRODUCTION TO THE DISABILITY

Music has been a component of the curriculum at schools for the blind for many years. The emphasis of these music programs has been to prompt the development of musical skills by the severely visually impaired, but otherwise, by able children who have traditionally been served in these residential centers. The introduction of "music for therapy" into these primarily "music for aesthetics" programs breaks the tradition of "music for music's sake." Although many administrators continue to expect musical excellence within their programs, some now support the use of music to promote cognitive, affective, and motor learning, often considered to be outside the instructional domain of the musician. Music is now used frequently within these centers to prompt nonmusical and musical behavior in children whose progress is below their ability when exposed only to traditional learning models. Music serves as an essential tool to teach these children necessary life skills without sacrificing their experience of music for pleasure. With this expanded mission, music continues to meet the educational needs of children in residential schools for the blind, which have served for many years as the primary learning centers for these students.

Music programs in residential centers were significantly affected by the implementation of Public Law 94-142, *The Education for All Handicapped Children Act of 1975.* This legislation defined the educational rights of handicapped children and mandated that they be educated by the states in the environment "least restrictive" to their total human needs (*Federal Register,* 1977). It provided the rationale for funds for programs, personnel, and adaptation of learning materials for special education, and "related services." It led to the educational placement of children according to need and ability, as well as disability. The implementation of PL 94-142 led to a more substantial integration of less severely disabled children with nonhandicapped children in public schools and the admission into residential schools of more multihandicapped, legally blind children. This change in enrollment left many music educators in residential centers lacking student musicians to serve their long established and often acclaimed vocal and instrumental groups. It provided an open door to music therapists who could teach music skills *and* shape the more basic cognitive, affective, motor, and social development of the partially disabled child.

In this monograph, the aim is to provide the music therapist and others with a resource for use in programs which serve severely visually impaired, and sometimes multihandicapped children. The monograph is also designed to meet the needs of educators in music therapy. The primary focus will be to introduce characteristics of the disability and to provide guidelines for use in teaching necessary skills to the visually disabled child. However, the discussion briefly considers the needs of the multihandicapped and deaf-blind child without necessarily referring to any additional disabilities. A detailed case study by Doreen Veazie-Desmangles, RMT, exemplifies a realistic profile of a multihandicapped youth involved in music therapy. Although written with the needs of children and adolescents in mind, this material should also prove useful to therapists working with severely visually impaired and/or multihandicapped adults. In this monograph, then, an attempt has been made to (a) describe the characteristics and needs of severely visually impaired children, (b) discuss the use of music as therapy/education in serving these children, (c) provide a case study representative of a multihandicapped visually impaired youth, and (d) suggest guidelines and materials for use in the development and maintenance of such a program.

CHARACTERISTICS OF THE DISABILITY

Definitions and Classifications

A common misconception exists that the term *blindness* refers only to individuals who exhibit total absence of visual capability at birth or who lose all vision sometime after birth (Meyen, 1978). Generally, the term *blind* refers to *legally blind* persons who may be totally blind or who may possess enough remaining vision to read printed matter with or without optical aids. Legally blind individuals are considered *congenitally disabled* when a severe dysfunction occurs after birth. Both the degree of vision loss and the effect of the disorder vary greatly among individuals. Special educators often avoid the misnomers associated with the legal blindness definition by referring to visually disabled individuals as being *severely visually impaired*. This description is inclusive of *low vision* or *partially sighted* persons as well as those who are totally blind (Cartwright & Cartwright, 1980).

There is a wide variety of visual disabilities within the blind population. While the types of defects vary from child to child, either acuity of vision or field of vision, or both, are affected. *Acuity* refers to how clearly something is seen. *Field* describes how much area the eye sees centrally and peripherally. An eye impairment may affect the *central* or reading vision and/or the *peripheral* or outer limits of vision which subtends approximately 180 degrees. Visual impairment may also include conditions which distort color vision or contribute to an imbalance of the external muscles of the eye (Lowenfeld, 1973).

Numerous organizations have developed definitions of visual disability to establish criteria for eligibility of special services to the handicapped. In 1934, the American Medical Association (AMA) defined blindness in terms of visual acuity (Harley, 1979). According to the AMA, a person is considered legally blind if his central visual acuity is 20/200 or less in the better eye with correction, or his peripheral visual field is so constricted that the widest diameter of such a field subtends an angle of distance no greater than 20 degrees (Meyen, 1978). A distance measure of 20/200 means that the visually impaired child sees with correction at 20 feet what the child with average vision of 20/20 is able to see at 200 feet. The AMA definition became the legal definition of blindness through the *Social Security Act of 1935*. The AMA parameters still serve as guidelines for the provision of government programs to visually disabled persons (Harley, 1979). *The Snellen Visual Acuity Test* is probably the most commonly used measure of visual acuity. The test consists of a number of letters or other shapes placed at a distance of 20 feet which must be identified by the reader (Cartwright & Cartwright, 1980). Results of the exam are reported in fractional terms and are easily compared to the AMA blindness parameters.

A legal definition of *partially seeing* was adopted by some states after 1935 (Harley, 1979). The purpose of this definition was to establish criteria for the eligibility of visually impaired children to receive special education services. *Partially seeing* children were defined as those children whose remaining visual acuity was greater than 20/200, but not greater than 20/70 in the better eye with correction (Cartwright & Cartwright, 1980). The 20/200 Snellen distance measurement was established as the boundary which divided children into blind and partially seeing groups. This "score" determined whether a child would be taught to read braille or print, whether he would learn primarily by tactile cues or by visual cues (Lowenfeld, 1973). Use of the Snellen distance measurement for this purpose has frequently been questioned as it considers the child's far distance functioning (at 20 feet) rather than his near distance capabilities. Near distance measures seem more suited to the determination of the child's primary learning medium as they consider the child's near task abilities. Reading and object manipulation are near distance tasks.

A recent medical-legal definition of blindness was established by the World Health Organization which categorized three ranges of visual potential in terms of distance.

These ranges included, (a) *blindness* which is defined as 20/500 or less, (b) *low vision* of 20/500 to 20/80 in the best eye with correction. In 1974, the United States Office of Education personnel and a National Advisory Committee from educational organizations functionally defined blind children as "sightless or having such limited vision that they must rely on hearing and touch as their chief means of learning," and functionally defined *partially seeing* children as "having severely impaired vision, but with enough residual vision with correction as to enable their primary learning medium to be printed matter" (Harley, 1979, p. 5). These additional definitions represented a move toward more useful near distance measures of vision.

The redefinition of terms indicated a change in educational thought away from near total reliance upon medical definitions to include reliance upon direct observation of the child by classroom teachers. The trend in special education is to replace the terms *blind* and *partially seeing* with terms which more exactly described the child's visual functioning, such as visual disability, visual impairment, and/or visual handicap. A child with a *visual disability* "differs from the average to such a degree that special personnel, curriculum adaptation, and/or additional instructional materials are needed to assist him in achieving at a level commensurate with his abilities." A *visual impairment* is regarded as "measurable physiological or functional loss of vision which could be described as deviation or departure from normalcy" (Harley, 1979, p. 4). A *visual handicap* may be regarded as any impairment severe enough to negatively effect a child's performance in areas such as reading or mobility. These definitions provide for more accurate diagnosis and educational placement of children by allowing for more precise measure of visual functioning. Whether a visual disability is perceived as a handicapping condition often depends upon the social reaction to the impairment. Visual disability remains one of the most devastating handicapping conditions in our society because of the nonsupportive behavior exhibited by parents, teachers, employers, and other members of the community.

Descriptive labels such as those discussed should be assigned to individuals only when necessary in establishing client eligibility for educational or medical services. It is appropriate for professionals to describe children in terms of abilities rather than disabilities. A child might be considered a "braille reader" or a "cane traveler" rather than a "blind child" (Harley, 1979). It is appropriate, when considering the abilities of handicapped persons, to perceive the person much like "the glass" as "half full," rather than, "half empty."

Incidence of Blindness

It is difficult to determine the number of severely visually impaired children in the United States. Discrepancy among disability definitions make it almost impossible to collect meaningful data concerning the incidence of severe eye disorder. As a result, actual figures vary significantly among agencies. The National Advisory Committee on Education of the Handicapped estimated in 1976 that the number of visually impaired children from 0 to 19 years of age numbered 66,000. A 1976 census by the American Printing House for the Blind (APHB) indicated that 28,995 legally blind children were enrolled in formal education programs through grade 12. Of these 28,995 children, 6,200 were braille readers, 12,426 read large print, 1,104 read both media, and 9,265 children were nonreaders. The total group included 1,234 deaf-blind students (Nolan, 1978, p. 412). The Printing House census excluded children not registered by the facility for federal assistance for instructional materials. These figures also excluded adults, as this population is generally not served by the APHB.

An analysis of existing data led Harley (1979) to conclude that severe visual disability accounts for a very small percentage of handicapped children, but for a very large percentage of handicapped adults. He indicated that, while many children receive professional eye care to correct visual distortion, relatively few are referred to special education programs. Printing House figures over several years seem to indicate that the number of legally blind children who read print has increased while the number of braille readers has consistently decreased since a 1977 registration. These figures suggest a significant increase in the number of nonreading visually impaired children receiving services from the American Printing House for the Blind. This increase parallels the noticeable rise in the number of multihandicapped children who are participating in ungraded classrooms. This trend might also account for a portion of the decrease in the numbers of braille readers. The number of nonreading, multihandicapped children receiving educational services has increased in recent years as a result of legislation on their behalf. Adults have also experienced the benefits of laws enacted for the handicapped. However, the frequent review and revision by legislators of laws which provide necessary services to the handicapped is a reminder that these services should not be taken for granted by concerned professionals.

The Eye and Common Impairments

A basic knowledge of the eye is essential in understanding the cause of blindness. A complex discussion of eye anatomy (see Figure 1) is not necessary for the purposes of this monograph, however, the following information is offered as a review of basic eye functions. Related disorders are included in the discussion.

The human eye is a complex sensory mechanism which receives visual imagery by virtue of light emitted by or reflected in the environment. It receives visual imagery to be interpreted by brain cells. Functional components of the visual system can be classified by function into four divisions: (1) protective, (2) refractive, (3) directive, and (4) receptive structures (Harley, 1979).

The protective structures of the eye consist of the orbit, orbital fat, eyelids, eyelashes, eyebrows, and tears. These components function to protect the eye against injury. The *orbit* is the bony cavity which surrounds the eyeball. A fatty tissue called the *orbital fat* cushions the eyeball and adjoining muscles and allows for the smooth rotation of the eye within the orbit. The *eyelashes* and *eyelids* guard the eyeball from harmful environmental agents, while *tears* moisten the surface of the eyeball (Vaughan, 1968). The *conjunctiva* is the lining of the eyelid. The primary disorders of the external eye are those which involve the conjunctiva (Harley & Lawrence, 1977). This group of disorders is generally referred to as *conjunctivitis* and includes infections such as "pink eye" and *gonococcal conjunctivitis*. These disturbances may generally occur at any age. For example, gonococcal conjunctivitis sometimes occurs in newborn infants as the result of contamination of the eyes during birth (Harley & Lawrence, 1977).

The refractive structures of the eye provide for the focusing of light necessary for vision. These include the retina, cornea, aqueous humor, lens, and vitreous body (Harley, 1979). The *retina* is the photoreceptive portion of the eye, which converts light into chemical energy and transmits visual messages to the brain through the optic nerve. The retina is the "ultimate sight for the focused image" (Harley & Lawrence, 1977, p. 44). The *cornea* is the transparent window of the eyeball which covers the iris or pigmented portion of the eye. Light must pass through the cornea before a visual image can form on the retina (Cartwright & Cartwright, 1980). The *lens* is a transparent body within the eyeball behind the pupil and iris of the eye. It focuses light rays on the light sensitive retina (Harley & Lawrence, 1977). The colorless fluid which is secreted posteriorly to the iris by the ciliary body to keep the globe of the eye firm is known as the *aqueous humor*. The *vitreous body* is a jelly-like substance which fills the eyeball and keeps the retina in place within the eye.

Diseases of the retina are common causes of blindness. These conditions may affect the reception and transmission of visual stimuli. Hemorrhages, extra-cellular fluid (edema),

FIGURE 1
Three-Dimensional Diagram of the Eye

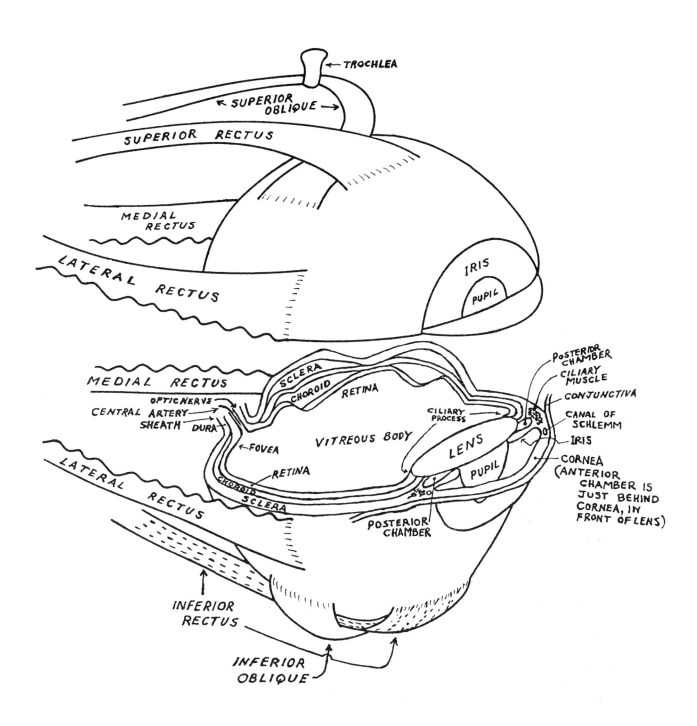

inflammation, cell degeneration, and tumors are common causes of retinal dysfunction. Blindness may result from diseased blood vessels which are associated with anemia, leukemia, kidney disease, diabetes, and high blood pressure. Retinitis pigmentosa and detachment of the retina are common retinal disorders. *Retinitis pigmentosa* is hereditary degeneration and atrophy of the retina. It is indicated by displaced pigment. *Detachment of the retina* is a separation of the retina by fluid from the overlying choroid tissue. The *choroid* is the vascular, pigmented middle layer of the posterior segment of the eye (Harley & Lawrence, 1977).

Common refractive abnormalities which involve other inclusive structures include corneal disorders, lens disorders, and disorders of eye shape and eye pressure. Corneal disorders include *keratitis,* or inflammation of the cornea, and *corneal degenerations* which are disturbances in cell growth. *Cataracts* are lens disorders which affect the focusing of light in the eye by covering the lens with an opaque substance (Cartwright & Cartwright, 1980). This condition may be hereditary or the result of rubella, Down's syndrome, or diabetes (Harley, 1979). Children as well as adults are susceptible to cataract conditions. *Myopia,* or extreme nearsightedness, results from refractive error usually caused by severe elongation of the eyeball. The resulting displacement of the lens too far from the retina causes inaccurate focusing of light. *Glaucoma* is a group of conditions caused by abnormal pressure buildup of the aqueous fluid of the eye (Harley, 1979; Harley & Lawrence, 1977). it may lead to gradual loss of sight by progressively increased distortion in the focusing of light by the eye. Glaucoma may be treated by chemotherapy and, in many cases, may not result in blindness.

The directive tissues of the visual system are six extraocular, voluntary muscles which move the eyes on an axis up, down, and to either side (Harley, 1979). These muscles include the *medial rectus* which moves the eye toward the nose and the *lateral rectus* which moves the eyes outward from the nose. Movement of the eyes up and down is facilitated by the combined actions of the *superior rectus* and *inferior oblique* muscles, and by the *inferior rectus* and the *superior oblique* muscles respectively (Vaughan, 1968). Directive disorders may accompany protective, refractive, and receptive disorders which sometimes weaken these adjoining muscles. *Strabismus,* or "crossed-eyes," is a disorder which affects coordination such that both eyes cannot be focused simultaneously on the same point at the same time. *Nystagmus* is a muscle dysfunction characterized by rapid, involuntary movement of the eyeball. This condition commonly accompanies other eye disorders and symptoms may increase during periods of stress (Harley, 1979; Cartwright & Cartwright, 1980).

The receptive tissues include the retina, the optic nerve, and the sensory area of the brain where visual perception occurs (Harley & Lawrence, 1977). Disorders of these areas may be due to pressure induced by tumor or cell degeneration caused by leukemia, blood clot, or injuries resulting from severe trauma to the head. Eye disorders involving receptive tissue include retinitis pigmentosa, optic atrophy, and retrolental fibroplasia (RLF). *Retinitis pigmentosa* was discussed as a refractive disorder. *Optic atrophy* involves the degeneration of nerve fibers which connect the retina of the eye to the cells of the brain; this condition results in difficulty interpreting visual stimuli. Retinitis pigmentosa and optic atrophy are common receptive disorders. *Retrolental fibroplasia* is no longer a common eye disorder in the United States. It is a condition of the retina, which causes blindness as the result of damage to the eye caused by excessive amounts of oxygen administered to prematurely born infants while in the incubator. This condition occurred somewhat frequently prior to improvements made in the treatment of these babies.

An eye disorder may be a *stable* condition as in total congenital blindness, or it may be a *progressive* disorder as in glaucoma. The nature of the condition is a variable to be considered in the definition of treatment, limitation of physical activity, and educational placement. When considering treatment possibilities, the stability of an eye condition might determine whether surgery is advisable or whether contact lenses are indicated. Eye stability may effect a child's ability to participate in some physical activity; for example, a child with progressive glaucoma may be advised not to participate in activities which frequently place the head below the waist area as this leads to added pressure to the eye. A person prone to detachment of the retina may be discouraged from activities which might result in even minor trauma to the head. The stability of the eye condition also should be considered when determining a child's primary learning medium. A child with some remaining vision, but who suffers from a progressive disorder that will probably result in functional blindness, should probably become a braille reader rather than a print reader, even while vision remains.

Identification of Eye Disorders

Children preparing for entry into educational programs are generally screened by school personnel or by the family physician for symptoms of eye dysfunction. The purpose of visual screening is to find those children who may suffer from eye or vision problems. These children are then referred for a professional eye examination. The initial screening procedure provides for gross identification only (Cartwright & Cartwright, 1980).

Generally, vision screening tests fall into two categories which include (a) those tests requiring specialized equipment or charts not normally found in regular classrooms, and (b) those tests which can be given without special materials (Cartwright & Cartwright, 1980). Procedures which test for visual acuity generally require special materials, while tests of muscular control and balance do not require special materials. There are no exceptions. Tests requiring special materials include (a) the *Snellen Visual Acuity Test,* (b) the *Snellen Test for Hyperopia, (c) the Prism Test for Binocular Awareness,* and (d) the *Pseudo-isochromatic Color Plates.* The *Snellen Visual Acuity Test* is the most widely known test of visual acuity. This test is sometimes called the Snellen Test for Hyperopia (farsightedness), as farsightedness can be detected during the screening for visual acuity. To take this test, an individual is asked to view the Snellen Chart through a pair of +2.5 diopter lenses. A child who *can* identify 4 of 6 symbols at a distance of 20 feet demonstrates acceptable visual acuity and passes the test. A child using the lenses who *cannot* see the specified number of symbols at the same distance demonstrates questionable visual acuity and fails the test. This child probably has hyperopia and should be referred for further testing. The *Prism Test for Binocular Awareness* tests how well both eyes work together to form a single image. In this test, a prism is held in front of one eye. The child focuses upon another object with the other eye. A child who can see the two objects at once demonstrates acceptable binocular functioning ability. A common test to measure color-blindness is the *Pseudo-isochromatic Plate Test.* To complete the exam, the child must read the numbers on 14 isochromatic plates which display one color imposed upon a background of another color. The child fails the test if he fails to recognize more than two numbers. The *Pseudo-isochromatic Color Plates* are frequently used to test color-blindness in adults qualifying for a driver's license (Cartwright & Cartwright, 1980).

The second category of visual screening measures are those which do not necessarily involve special materials. These are informal measures which involve observation of the child's eye condition and his behavior within his usual learning environment. Indicators of possible eye disorders might include notice of (a) red or swollen eyelids, (b) crusts or discharges on the eyelids or among eyelashes, (c) inflamed or watery eyes, (d) crossed eyes, (e) repeated sties, (f) drooping lids, (g) dilated eyes, or (h) oscillating eyes. Unusual behavior should also be noted and reported to medical personnel and the child's parents. Behaviors denoting possible eye dysfunction include (a) squinting, (b) excessive rubbing of the eyes, (c) frequent thrusting of the head in a forward direction, (d) any lack of coordination in the simultaneous focusing of both eyes, and (d) excessive blinking behavior. A child might give clues to eye disorder in reporting (a) difficulty in reading a chalkboard, (b) difficulty in reading from a book at a "normal" distance, (c) blurred vision, (d) itching eyes, and (e) burning eyes. A child may demonstrate symptoms of disorder if he (a) is behind his class in reading, (b) loses his place while reading, (c) skips or re-reads lines, (d) vocalizes when reading silently, (e) reverses or confuses letters or words, (f) tilts his head or covers one eye while reading, and (g) uses his finger as a marker while reading (Cartwright & Cartwright, 1980; Harley, 1979). Frequent dizziness, headaches, or nausea which occur following the completion of near distance tasks might also be symptomatic of visual dysfunction.

Eye Care and Other Vision Specialists

An *ophthalmologist, or oculist,* is a medical doctor who specializes in the detection and treatment of diseases and defects of the eye. The physician is licensed to perform surgery and to prescribe medication and alternative treatments to improve effective eye use. Treatment possibilities include the prescription of corrective lenses (Cartwright & Cartwright, 1980; Lowenfeld, 1973).

An *optometrist* is a nonmedical practitioner trained to test eye functioning; that is, he measures refractive errors such as irregularities in the size or shape of the eyeball or cornea, and assesses eye muscle disturbances. He is licensed to correct visual difficulties through the prescription of corrective lenses and eye exercises only. An *optician* prepares corrective lenses once they have been prescribed. He custom grinds lenses, fits them in frames, and adjusts glasses to the individual wearer (Cartwright & Cartwright, 1980; Lowenfeld, 1973).

A *peripathologist* is an educator who works primarily with totally blind persons to facilitate improved space orientation and mobility skills. He is trained to teach skills necessary to effect movement through space, which include, but are not limited to, part and whole body awareness, sensory motor perception, awareness of distance and direction, and problem-solving skills related to mobility. The peripathologist teaches travel and pre-travel skills to blind individuals, and sometimes teaches travel with the use of a seeing eye dog but more often teaches cane travel. The peripathologist is more commonly called an "orientation and mobility instructor."

Special educators are teachers certified to provide instruction to handicapped children. These professionals are trained in the techniques, materials and equipment useful to students with visual disabilities and possibly multihandicapped conditions. They are aware of the curriculum adaptations needed to facilitate successful learning behavior by these children. The type and amount of aid provided by these teachers varies according to job description. Qualified special educators include the special teacher, the itinerant teacher, and the consulting teacher. The *special teacher* is certified to teach exceptional children, usually within a self-contained classroom. The "exceptional" child may be gifted as well as handicapped in his abilities. The *itinerant teacher* provides direct service to the handicapped child, but generally does not preside over a classroom of students; he works in close cooperation with the child's classroom teacher and tutors the child on an individual basis. The *consulting teacher* does not provide direct services to the handicapped child, but instead, serves as a resource to teachers who work directly with the child. He may provide useful techniques to the classroom teacher or suggest materials for use in instruction of the visually impaired child. The job descriptions of the itinerant and consulting teachers sometimes overlap as the itinerant teacher may serve both roles within a given school system. Teachers and therapists with intensive training in the needs of severely visually impaired children often serve as their primary educators. However, the migration of capable visually impaired students away from residential facilities to traditional public schools means that more special educators will serve as support personnel rather than primary educators to these less disabled children.

Educational Placement

Severely visually impaired children may receive educational services in a number of instructional settings. These educational environments may be ranked from that which is least "adapted" to the child's disability, to that which is most "adapted" to his special needs. The *traditional classroom* environment may be least adapted to the needs of the visually impaired student. In this public school setting, the child participates in all classroom activities and functions at grade level. He remains with his classmates throughout the school day, and may receive little or no additional help from a special educator. Students placed in this setting must demonstrate competence in all necessary special skill areas and be able to adapt to the "sighted" classroom.

A slightly adapted version of the traditional classroom setting is the *public school classroom with itinerant teacher support*. The child in this placement remains in the traditional classroom, but receives additional services from a specially trained teacher-consultant when indicated. This traveling, or itinerant, teacher circulates from school to school to provide special services to schools which serve visually disabled children. He may assist the child directly or indirectly, by providing assistance to the classroom teacher. Direct service would include the adaptation of learning materials (i.e., large print or braille texts, optical aids), and instruction in the use of materials as necessary. Services to the teacher might include instruction in developing methods and materials for use by the visually impaired child within the traditional setting.

The *public school classroom with resource room support* is a more "adapted" educational environment. The child in this placement remains with his classmates for much of the school day. However, he leaves the classroom on a regular basis to receive more direct instruction from a special educator in a classroom for disabled children. During these special sessions, the child is tutored in class subjects and learning materials as necessary.

The *self-contained classroom* provides a setting for special instruction throughout the school day to handicapped children. Children who are often well below grade level academically and who require an adapted curriculum are assigned to the self-contained learning center. The child is generally encouraged to participate with children outside his classroom in the social environment provided by the public school system. This child is placed in the public school to participate in a learning environment which is least restrictive to his total development; but which provides for his special needs as well.

Children who will benefit from an educational program developed to address the needs of the severely visually impaired and often multihandicapped child might attend a *residential school* to receive these special services. The residential school receives public funds, but is a self-contained school for children whose primary disability is of a visual nature. In addition, these facilities provide housing for their students, as many children must travel some distance from home to attend these schools. Generally, to be served by a state operated residential school, a child must be considered legally blind.

Some children receive *homebound instruction*. When a child is unable to function successfully in the social and academic structure provided by the classroom, he may receive the services of an itinerant teacher who travels to the child's home, to work with the child on an individual basis. In addition, the itinerant teacher involves the parents in the training so that instruction can continue when he is unavailable. Those who receive homebound services are primarily severely/profoundly handicapped children who are so defined by law, when they demonstrate two or more primary handicapping conditions.

Recent legislation concerning education for handicapped children mandates that a child be reevaluated on a regular basis to assure that his current educational placement is most conducive to his total development. A handicapped child may be moved from one educational environment to another as appropriate to facilitate the child's progress.

Growth and Development

The development of the severely visually impaired and the totally blind child is more similar than dissimilar to that of the normally sighted child. The visually impaired child progresses through the same developmental sequence as any other child, but his progress may be slower due to conditions directly or indirectly related to his visual disability (Lowenfeld, 1973). Variables which directly retard development are the immediate result of lack of vision. To offset the devastating effects of visual loss, the child must participate in numerous compensatory experiences. Activities common to the experience of sighted children must be implanted into the daily routine of the visually impaired child; for example, lack of vision directly impedes a child's effectiveness in establishing and maintaining early primary relationships with significant others. Concrete experiences which nurture early social skills must be included in daily activities. The visually impaired child is further restricted in his desire and ability to move within and explore his immediate environment. He must constantly be encouraged to interact with the people, places, and objects which surround him. The blind child should receive approval for his exploratory behavior until the exploration becomes its own reward.

Variables which indirectly affect the child's development are environmental restrictions which are externally imposed upon the child because of his disability. Sighted community members often interact with the visually impaired individual according to stereotypic preconceptions of the child's disability. These interactions limit the child's ability to function as independently as possible in the "sighted world." The blind child must be provided experiences which will encourage feelings of self-worth. Direct and indirect influences affecting the behavior of the visually impaired child often overlap by definition, but it is essential to recognize that both exist. It is also essential to provide the child with concrete growth experiences which will enable him to compensate for the effects of his handicap and nurture his growth in all developmental areas (Lowenfeld, 1973). Severely visually impaired children and sighted children progress through an equivalent developmental sequence (see the works of Piaget). The rate of growth varies among all children regardless of disability and among visually impaired children whose abilities likewise vary. However, with these disclaimers, some comparisons between sighted and severely visually impaired children are indicated.

Comparison of growth patterns of groups of visually impaired, but otherwise non-handicapped students, with normally sighted children indicate that the academically competent blind child will begin, and often remain, one or two years below grade level in some areas of learning (Lowenfeld, 1973). Figure 2 provides a sample developmental profile of a ten-year-old severely visually impaired child in grade five. The child described is of average height and weight for his age. His speech and language development represent grade level functioning. He is slightly below grade level in mental age and well below grade (age) level in motor coordination, social maturity, and academic skills which require symbolization and reasoning skills. Severely visually impaired children generally demonstrate difficulty completing tasks which require synthesis of information into a concept of "whole," generalization about objects or ideas, and abstract (versus concrete) cognitive analysis. This profile is representative of many severely visually handicapped children in academic programs.

Stress and Behavior

An affliction which affects a child affects the *whole* child. Any treatment must consider the whole child as well. In 1956, Selye introduced to the medical world a conceptual model of illness, which defined it and traced the interdependence of factors which contribute to ill health. His theory provides insight into the behavior of the handicapped child, as it considers the child's disability within the perspective of his total life experience. Michel (1976) presents a diagram (see Figure 3) based on Selye's concept of stress, which alludes to the role of therapy in the treatment of the whole child.

FIGURE 2
Developmental Chart

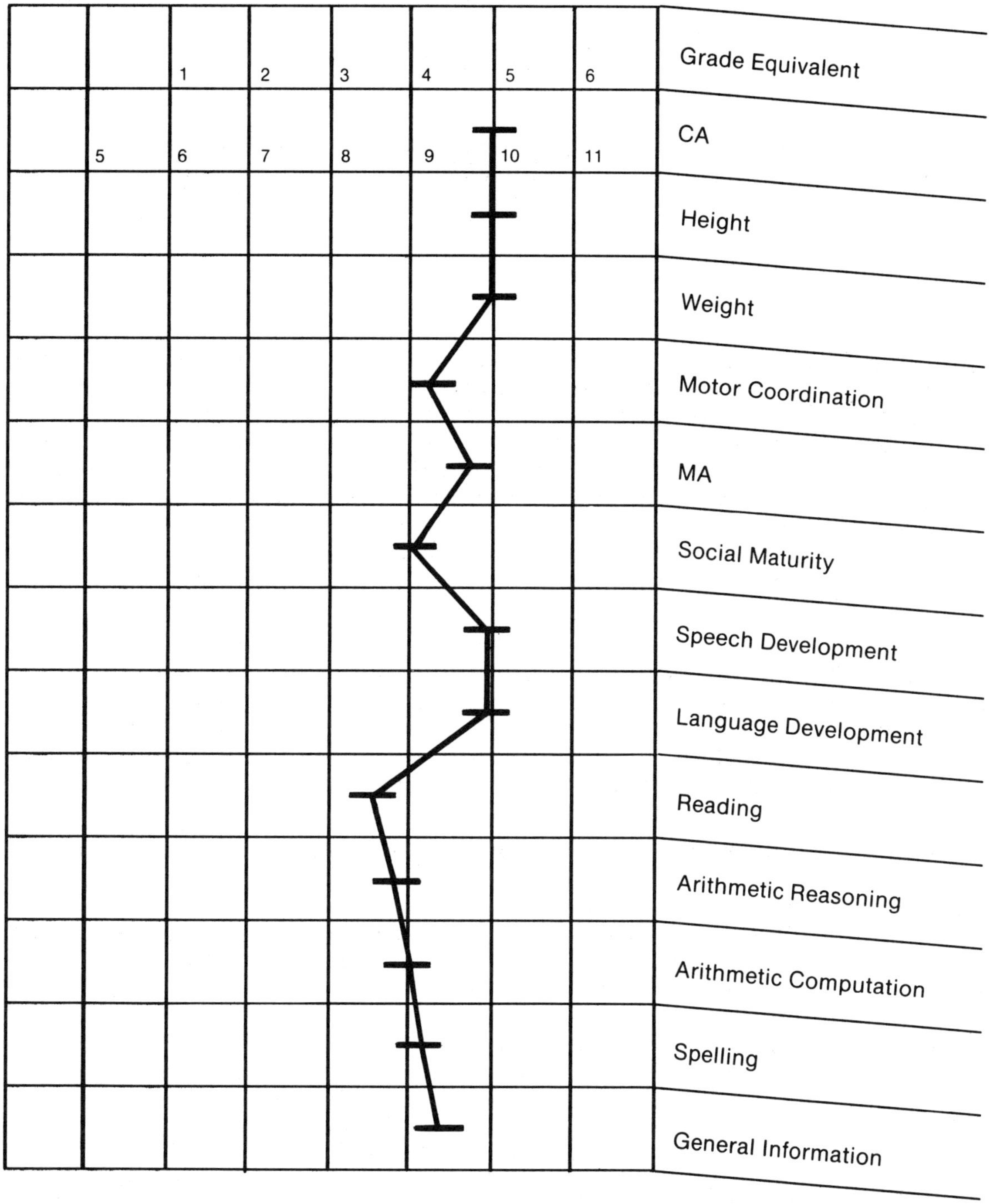

		1	2	3	4	5	6	Grade Equivalent
	5	6	7	8	9	10	11	CA
								Height
								Weight
								Motor Coordination
								MA
								Social Maturity
								Speech Development
								Language Development
								Reading
								Arithmetic Reasoning
								Arithmetic Computation
								Spelling
								General Information

FIGURE 3
Concept of Illness

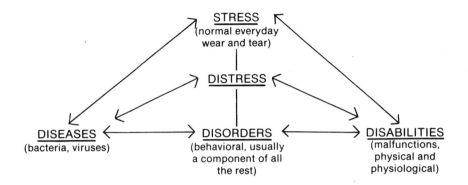

Selye lists the components of illness as (a) *stress* which is common daily "wear and tear" which results from the pressures of daily life, (b) *distress* which is the individual's inability to cope successfully with persons or events causing stress, (c) *disorders* which are frequently manifested socially inappropriate behavior patterns that may be symptomatic of emotional ill health, (d) *disabilities* which are intellectual, emotional, and/or physical conditions severe enough to significantly reduce the success with which an individual functions, and (e) *diseases* which are debilitating physical conditions influenced by stressful environmental stimuli. Selye defines these terms as related components which affect human intellectual, emotional, and physical functioning (Michel, 1976; Selye, 1956).

Selye defines *health* as a state of equilibrium or balance between opposing forces. Stressful stimuli must be balanced by an individual's ability to successfully cope with the stress causing experience. Selye defines *ill health* as a state of disequilibrium or imbalance in which an individual is unable to cope with stress. He indicates that a state of ill health is the direct result of lack of fulfillment of human needs. Stress, distress, disorder, disability, and disease are factors which may adversely affect communicative, academic, motor, and social-emotional behavior.

A child may conceptually enter Selye's model from any point and may progress to any other point in the diagram as indicated by the arrows which connect the words; for example, a severely visually impaired child would generally enter the diagram at the disability level. If his blindness is adventitiously acquired, he will usually suffer distress in adapting to his handicapping condition. This newly blinded child may have been well-adjusted and orderly in his sighted classroom, but may exhibit disruptive or withdrawn behavior when placed in a classroom for visually impaired children. Should this behavior become consistently severe over time, the child might be considered characteristically as exhibiting a behavioral disorder. If his health deteriorates during this process, he may become more susceptible to disease, adding to his distress. Disability, disorder, and disease are variables which may easily magnify the child's perception of stress and impair his emotional, social, and economic development.

Attempting to define the role of music therapy in education and rehabilitation, Sears (1968) indicates that desirable changes in behavior may result (a) from cognitive and physical responses elicited by paired association with the music itself, (b) by active listening to music, (c) by having music in the environment as background, and (d) in the making of music. Although music therapists cannot change a child's past experiences,

Sears specifies that they can "organize a *present* situation so that the *effect of the past* is altered for a more adequate *future*" (p. 32). Music may provide a healthy environment, an activity conducive to learning, and serve as a means of reinforcing goal-directed behavior of children receiving services.

Sears (1968) also identifies three constructs which exemplify the processes through which music therapy brings about desirable behavioral change. The environment provided in music therapy promotes human experience (a) *within structure,* (b) *in self-organization,* and (c) *in relating to others.* Accordingly, participation in music therapy promotes individual growth in the following ways:

1. Music provides for experience within structure. Music demands that the child respond within limits of time, ability, and at activity-appropriate emotional response levels. In music therapy, a child must (a) maintain contact with reality and (b) remain on task for the duration of a given activity. Music activities are structured to accommodate the cognitive and physical response levels of each child. These activities promote sensory-elaborated behavior by demanding that the child focus upon, discriminate among, and respond appropriately to perceived sensory stimuli of all types. In activities structured to promote nonmusic learning, music may also elicit extramusical ideas and associations. Music may easily be incorporated into activities designed to teach emotional, communicative, motor, social, and academic skills (Lathom, 1980).

2. Music provides for experience in self-organization. Music promotes self-expression at preverbal, nonverbal, and verbal levels of communication. Music provides a medium through which the handicapped child can compensate for behavior which is considered below age level functioning. The handicapped child can often participate in music activities at a level which is equivalent to or which surpasses the ability level of the non-disabled child. Participation in group music activities can promote feelings of success and pride in self, and can provide opportunities for socially acceptable experiences of reward and nonreward. The experience of group music activity by the handicapped child provides an arena in which he can feel needed by others and know their personal interest and support.

3. Music provides for experience in relating to others. Music provides a socially acceptable medium for self-expression at nonverbal and verbal expressive levels. Within groups, music provides the individual with opportunities to accept responsibility. The child must be responsible for his own behavior and, to some degree, for that of the group as a whole. He must practice self-directed behavior and develop skills to enable the direction of others when serving in a leadership role. When a child participates in group activities, he must learn and practice a variety of communication skills. He learns pride in self. He learns to identify with the group and to suppress his needs for the benefit of the group. Group music activity provides a realistic structure for the practice of necessary social skills.

According to Duerkson (1978), music may be used in therapy with children in a variety of ways. It serves as a *carrier of information* when song lyrics are used to attract and maintain the child's attention while presenting pertinent information. Song lyrics might convey information about animals, colors, numbers, seasons, etc. Music may be used as a *reinforcer* when the child's participation in a desired musical activity is contingent upon the elicitation of specific nonmusic behavior; for example, a child might trade tokens earned for initiating verbalization for time used in playing his favorite instrument. Music may be used as a *background for learning* when music sets the mood for an activity, such as exercise or relaxation. It serves as a *physical structure for learning* when music is used to actively direct behavior, as when body concepts are taught through lyrics which direct activity and require an immediate action response. For example, the therapist might direct the child by singing, "touch your fingers to your toes"; in this case, the music serves as the stimulus to prompt a specific action response. Music used as a physical structure for learning is different from music used as a carrier of information. In the latter function, song lyrics may demand no action other than listening. Words might identify common food groups and indicate specific foods that fit in each group. When music functions as a physical structure for learning in this same activity, the lyrics might direct the child to "name a fruit," or "name a vegetable." These two musical functions are often combined into a "listen and do" activity. Music is sometimes used as a *reflection of skills or processes to be learned.* When musical elements, such as tempo, dynamics, and pitch are isolated to teach corresponding nonmusical concepts ("fast-slow", "loud-soft", "high-low"), the musical concepts are reflective of nonmusical concepts to be learned. As always, music can be taught as a medium for aesthetic expression and for enjoyment of "music for music's sake." The experience of music for leisure or pleasure is still a primary function of musical stimuli.

Music activities for children may be categorized into (a) listening, (b) the making of music, (c) moving to music, and (d) musical games. *Listening* activities include passive listening for pleasure and instructional purposes, and active listening. A child required to listen in an active manner must focus his attention on a specific musical sound or selection to derive a desired meaning from it. Duerkson's use of music as a "reinforcer" or as "a background for learning" and Sear's "music itself" and "having music in the environment" are examples of passive listening. Duerkson's use of music as "a carrier of information," "a physical structure for learning," and as "a reflection of skills or processes to be learned" would involve the child in active listening. Active listening corresponds with Sear's definition of "listening to music."

The *making of music* includes both the re-creation of music written by others and the creation of original music by the child. Music-making activities might be used to reinforce nonmusic learning or to teach music skills and aesthetic appreciation. The making of music involves the initiation of vocal and/or instrumental responses by the child, either alone or with others. (Dance or movement might also be incorporated into the activity.) Making music enables the child to (a) respond to the musical environment with pleasure, (b) respond to the musical environment with success, (c) learn music skills for successful group participation, (d) invest in group music processes, and (e) apply individual and group music skills in new situations, often outside the music domain. These concepts draw heavily upon the Developmental Therapy Model of learning (Graham, 1975). Research in music therapy indicates that skills developed to function successfully in music activities also enable the child to function successfully in nonmusic experiences.

Activities which involve *moving to music* may be divided into (a) nonlocomotor movement, that is, movement within the child's personal space, (b) locomotor movement, that is, movement from his current position to his desired position in space, (c) gross motor or large muscle movement, and (d) fine motor or small muscle movement. Movement activities may be directed toward a specific body level to include the whole body or specific regions, such as the (a) head, (b) waist, (c) knees, and (d) toes. Proponents of Orff Schulwerk techniques teach muscial concepts and encourage creativity through (a) modeled and improvised movement and (b) vocal and instrumental "music-making." Using some of these techniques, a music therapist might conceptually divide the body into levels designating body parts to serve as specific "body instruments." A child's hand may "snap fingers" while positioned high in the head region. The child may "clap hands" at waist level, or "patsch" (pat knees with his palms) at knee level. He may "stamp feet" to encourage the use of the lower body. The child might be asked to combine movements across body levels. To do this, the therapist might model a rhythmic "patsch-clap" pattern with a given tempo and ask the child to imitate the pattern, or later, to participate in a call-response activity which requires simple improvisational skill. To improvise, the child uses a part of the "call" rhythm in his "response." To include the use of unpitched instruments and pitched instruments, such as the xylophones and metallophones, rhythms performed by specific body "instruments" may be transferred to the various instruments. For example, in common time, a series of quarter notes played as "patsch-clap-patsch-clap" on body instruments might become the tonic and dominant notes played on a xylophone as the bass part to a simple song. In this way, a "movement to music" activity (dance) becomes a "making of music" activity involving instruments. Movement to music is artistically defined as dance, and can be imitative or improvised by the child. It may involve only one child, a child and his partner, or a group of children depending upon the child's individual needs and abilities.

Musical games synthesize music-making activities and movement activities into play. Broadly defined, musical games include (a) traditional childhood folk games which incorporate rhythm and/or pitch into a movement activity, and (b) games developed or adapted by the therapist to teach necessary skills. Childhood folk games revolve around nursery rhymes and other folk chants. They include "jump rope games," "hot potato," and "ring-around-the-rosey." The folk heritage is rich and the repertoire seems endless. Some folk chants are commonly recited to two- or three-note melodic patterns. These simple pitch patterns serve as a natural beginning for the reinforcing pitch concepts. Games developed by therapists teach color concepts, number concepts, size and shape, etc. This repertoire is limited only to the degree that the therapist's creativity is limited.

When selecting activities to structure learning, the therapist must consider the role of music therapy in the child's total treatment plan. He must evaluate each child's present level of functioning, developmental history, educational goals, and leisure interests (Lathom, 1980). He must consider treatment limitations, such as therapist-client contact hours and size of the treatment group. Because the therapist is often limited to small group or large group access, the music therapist must usually plan his sessions around the combined needs of a group of children. Long-term goals should be reduced to short-term objectives and arranged progressively to enable the child to reach the desired goal. Goals and objectives should be stated in terms of observable (measurable) behavior, and activities should be developed to promote learning of the desired behavior. The child's abilities should be evaluated prior to, during, and at the cessation of treatment, to assess progress.

The role of music therapy and other therapies is to interrupt the cycle which Selye (1956) called "The Concept of Illness" by introducing structure which demands desirable behavior change. To do this, the therapist introduces a nurturing environment which is supportive of the child's needs but is demanding of behavior, in approximation, to the child's long-range ability. He continuously places the child in situations where (a) his inappropriate behavior is incompatible with completion of the given structured tasks, (b) desired behavior is modeled and then demonstrated by the child, and (c) inappropriate behavior is redirected and, therefore, extinguished. The therapist provides an environment for the child, which leads him from his immediate level of functioning to more functional behavioral patterns. An environment is structured which encourages the child to respond to external stimuli with pleasure and success. In addition, the therapist provides skills which must, in time, generalize to other environments.

Music therapy techniques are used to (a) teach the child to express emotion in socially acceptable forms, (b) improve self-concept through success oriented experiences, (c) develop skills which will enhance emotional, communicative, academic, motor, and social adaptation to his disability, and (d) develop musical skills for pleasure. In music therapy, the clinician observes, records, treats, and reevaluates the child's behavior throughout the therapeutic process in order to effectively teach skills which will ultimately enable the child to function more successfully, more enjoyably in his world. Selye's "Concept of Illness" need not represent the profile of every handicapped child, but it is the role of health-care personnel to promote self-acceptance by handicapped children and to facilitate the development of health coping skills to combat the ill effects of stress resulting from disease, disorder, or disability.

MUSIC THERAPY WITH CHILDREN

"Music is an essential . . . function of man. It influences his behavior and has done so for thousands of years" (Gaston, 1968, p. 7.) Music exists in all known cultures and influences persons of all ages. Music is important to our ritual, our leisure and more recently, to the educational development of our children. Educators continue to recognize the powerful effect of music in prompting or reinforcing desired nonmusic responses in children. This recognition has resulted in an increase in the number of music therapists serving in special education programs. Although music therapists have worked with handicapped children for a number of years, the passage of P L 94-142 by Congress officially mandated music therapy as a *related service* to be included in their educational programs (*Federal Register*, 1977).

Music therapy is the scientific application of music and the therapist's skills to bring about desirable changes in human behavior. Music therapy, as a discipline, draws from research and theories in music, the natural sciences, and particularly the behavioral sciences. The structure provided by the therapeutic environment and the relationship between therapist and child, child, and peers, facilitates the learning of necessary life skills. Children may learn skills which facilitate effective emotional, social, communicative, and academic functioning over time.

A useful model for teaching necessary life skills to children through music was developed by Purvis and Samet (1976) for use at Rutland Center in Athens, Georgia. Their text is based on the Developmental Therapy Model established by Mary Wood. It serves as an example of a behavior-based music therapy curriculum for therapeutic intervention with children who demonstrate maladaptive behavior and emotional disorder. In developmental music therapy, activities are designed to teach (a) behavior, (b) communication, (c) socialization, and (d) academics through structured (1) listening, (2) playing, (3) singing, (4) moving, (5) creating, and (6) verbalizing experiences. These activities teach skills identified with five progressive developmental therapy stages which include:

STAGE I: Responding to the Environment with Pleasure.
STAGE II: Responding to the Environment with Success.
STAGE III: Learning Skills for Successful Group Participation.
STAGE IV: Investing in Group Processes.
STAGE V: Applying Individual and Group Skills in New Situations.

For a more detailed description of the use of music in Developmental Therapy refer to *Music in Developmental Therapy: A Curriculum Guide* (Purvis & Samet, 1976) and *Developmental Music Therapy* (Purvis & Samet, 1974), both published by the National Association for Music Therapy. Further discussion of the use of music in developmental therapy is included in a chapter by Graham (1975) entitled, "Music Education of Emotionally Disturbed Children" in the text, *Music for the Exceptional Child*. The tenets of the developmental model can be located in expanded form in the books, *Developmental Therapy* (Wood, 1975), and *The Rutland Center Model for Treating Emotionally Disturbed Children* (Wood, 1972). These materials were created to meet the educational needs of emotionally disturbed children. However, the model is functional, and many of the activities are adaptable for use with severely visually impaired children.

Music provides an essential means of communication, and an effective learning medium for severely visually impaired children. These children rely heavily upon auditory cues to receive information from their environment. They must rely on information acquired by tactile exploration, muscle sense, smell, taste, and remaining vision to perceive and respond to objects and individuals. Music activities provide a structure to promote the synthesis of sensory information and allow for development of socially appropriate response skills. Further, participation in music activities allows the visually impaired child to perceive beauty through aesthetically pleasing experiences. Music therapy services should be an integral part of the education and rehabilitation of severely visually impaired persons.

Teaching Skills Through Music[1]

Music may be used to teach (a) communication skills, (b) academic skills, (c) motor skills, and (d) patterns for successful social-emotional interaction. The music therapist who chooses to teach visually impaired children must expand himself, his philosophy, and his teaching skills to be successful. He must learn to "think" in terms of each of his five senses, favoring none. He must develop an awareness which will enable him to see more clearly and express himself more accurately than he has previously. The therapist must be comfortable with himself. He must act with clarity and consistency when communicating with the child, and he must do so easily through nuances of touch, voice timbre and inflection, and movement. He must develop language to describe objects as easily in tactile terms as in visual terms. The music therapist must demonstrate the ability to communicate with the blind child so that the child knows, without benefit of visual cue, the message which is being conveyed to him.

Severely visually impaired children learn more successfully when they participate in multi-sensory instructional experiences. These children must be challenged to focus upon stimuli perceived through individual senses, and must learn to integrate simultaneously received information.

The music therapist must develop a creative arts approach to teaching necessary concepts. The child must experiment with musical instruments, learn to feel music through vibration as well as to hear music, and experience defined partial body and whole body movement to musical selections of various tempos and moods. The child should also paint to music with fingers and toes in order to feel art and music simultaneously; in short, he must learn to synthesize verbal and nonverbal forms of expression to communicate with others. The effective therapist will borrow techniques from drama experts and art and dance therapists to develop a curriculum which meets the communication, academic, motor, and creative means of self-expression. The music therapist should incorporate music into learning activities, but should not be limited by it!

The Music Program at Oak Hill School

Oak Hill School, conducted by the Connecticut Institute for the Blind, is a 12-month residential facility which offers services for children with multihandicaps through age 21. In keeping with the charter of the school, all the residents have visual impairments.

The program at Oak Hill stresses that learning takes place in the classroom as well as during all other daily activities. The uniqueness of the program maintains the philosophy that students should be provided with as many opportunities as possible which help them to experience a progressive series of "learning for life" levels: complete dependency, supervised self-help training, supervised semi-independent living, and supervised group home living. The opportunities for these experiences are conducted by professional and support staffs. In working with the student, there is on-going communication among therapists, teachers, and support staff to determine carry-over from one area of the program to another.

Because of the multiplicity of handicapping conditions among the students, the music therapy program at Oak Hill School has adopted a multi-sensory approach. Each student is evaluated to determine his needs, abilities, and limitations. A therapeutic program is established whereby these needs can be met and appropriate behavioral changes can take place through the student's experience with the elements of music: rhythm, pitch, timbre, and dynamics.

The four goal areas where music therapy is applied as a therapeutic agent are communication, academics, motor, and social/emotional growth. These goal areas are in keeping with Oak Hill's statement of policy as a residential program for the growth and development of the whole child.

Students are provided with opportunities to learn, develop, apply and consistently reinforce skills, attitudes and behaviors necessary for eventual placement in a highly structured living environment or in a supervised semi-independent residence and for successful participation in a sheltered workshop or a day activity program. Each student's program promotes development in the following areas:

1. Personal hygiene and health routines.
2. Management of personal possessions.
3. Care of clothing (maintaining neat closets and bureaus, washing, folding, etc.)
4. Dining skills and etiquette.
5. Simple light housekeeping.
6. Simple meal preparation and kitchen "know how."
7. Ability to move about freely and appropriately in a familiar environment.
8. Ability to accept and deal appropriately with environmental changes.
9. Reinforcement of pre-work and work activity skills.
10. Constructive use of leisure time, including the development and pursuit of individual hobbies and interests as well as participation in a wide variety of structured recreational activities.
11. Sense of security, belonging, acceptance, and comfort.
12. Sense of accomplishment in matters of task completion.
13. Ability to communicate needs effectively.
14. Cooperation with peers and/or staff.
15. Ability to interrelate with peers.
16. Ability to comply with the organized routine and suitable behaviors appropriate to group living and life style.
17. Development of individual preferences and opportunities to choose between two or more acceptable alternatives or to decline by indicating "no" (as appropriate).
18. Ability to differentiate coins, understand the use of money and manage money (as appropriate).
19. Promotion/maintenance of physical health, good muscle tone, body coordination, and manipulative/hand skills.
20. Opportunities to channel frustrations through acceptable outlets.

Bert: A Case Study[2]

Bert was a 20-year-old student whose primary disability was blindness abetted by severe/profound mental retardation. He had a double scoliosis but ambulated independently with a shuffled gait. Bert entered the 12-month residential program at the age of 18, at which time the teaching staff referred him to the music therapist. Through classroom consultation, the following observations were made: Bert would not become involved in any of the music activities presented. He refused to play rhythm instruments and either dropped them on the floor or threw them across the room. He preferred to sit on his hands and rock back and forth in a self-stimulating manner. He resisted gross motor movements which were done with hand-over-hand physical prompts. He clung to anyone near him whenever he was prompted to walk independently.

After Bert had been in the program for six months, he showed marked improvement in many areas. He was able to trail his way from the classroom to the dining room with just a frequent tap on the shoulder. He no longer sat on his hands but was willing to hold music instruments and attempt to play some of them. Live and vocal music brought about more appropriate responses even though his perseverated rocking continued whenever recorded music was played. He would smile at the therapist whenever familiar songs were sung, and he also began to vocalize on the sounds "s" and "sh." At this time an initial assessment (see Appendix A) was conducted to determine the appropriateness of music therapy in Bert's Individual Education Plan (IEP). In light of his adjustment to his new program and his appropriate responses to music, Bert was scheduled for therapy sessions three times a week for 15-minute periods. The purpose of the session was to increase receptive and expressive language and to improve mobility skills.

Bert's progress can be seen in the "Music Therapy Baseline Checklist" presented in Appendix B. After 12 months of therapy, Bert's strongest response to music was hand clapping on verbal cue and making some vocalizations with gutteral sounds. When he was praised for achieving a task during a music activity, he smiled and laughed to familiar music. His communication skills improved through auditory and/or tactile discrimination in his being able to "sign" for several instruments and activities including drum, tambourine, triangle, and dance. He was able to sign his preference when given a choice of gesture songs, and he would engage spontaneously in 80% of the gestures requested. He was able to distinguish number concepts by beating his full name on the triangle and a series of 3, 4, or 5 beats when asked to do so. His mobility improved in that he could trail a rope across the music therapy room toward the sound of music and away from the source with only verbal cues.

Bert's weakest area was his reluctance to try a new activity which involved creative movement. He was very hesitant about leaving his seat to dance or march. Also, he continued to be resistant to holding unfamiliar instruments and playing them without physical assistance from the therapist. Because music was a viable medium through which his education program could be carried out, it was recommended that he continue to receive direct services in individual therapy. He needed more work in spatial awareness, following 2-step commands, and spontaneity in instrument playing. The continued use of songs and activities would help to increase body awareness and improve his expressive language in making his needs known. Also, it was recommended by the physical therapist and orientation-mobility instructor that he continue to develop mobility skills while holding his head erect (he tended to let his head hang forward) through auditory discrimination activities, so that the curvature of his spine would be minimized.

After three months of working on his new objectives in music therapy, Bert was able to follow a 2-step command. Bert could distinguish between the sound of raindrops, which he played by tapping his right index finger to a tom-tom, and the sound of wind, which he made by rubbing his palm across the tom-tom and vocalizing "shwish." He could walk to recorded music while tapping rhythm sticks held by the therapist, and follow verbal commands for left/right and forward/backward concepts. At the same time, he could hold his head erect with only a verbal cue. He trailed a rope a distance of 20 feet across the room toward the source of music coming from the stereo; however, the rope was attached to a kettle drum on either end, so Bert held a mallet in one hand while trailing the rope with the other. Upon reaching the drum, he beat it with the mallet in time to the recorded music. He stopped when asked to do so, transferred the mallet to the other hand and trailed the rope with the opposite hand away from the source of music to the other kettle drum, and repeated his drum playing. Bert would be leaving the program at age 21. Because weaknesses were beginning to develop into strengths, he no longer was as resistive to exploring his environment; he was able to do so through auditory and tactile discrimination. He learned to express his likes and dislikes appropriately and to make his needs known through sign language and appropriate gestures.

Music therapy had a positive effect on Bert's educational program. The music therapy objectives were developed as part of a total program which viewed the child as a whole. Music therapy helped Bert to develop some of the skills and behaviors he would need for day activity center and semi-independent living settings. Because he was a potential candidate for a group home sponsored by Oak Hill, it was believed that Bert's interest in music would continue to be an important part of his life and his leisure time activities.

DEVELOPMENT OF COMMUNICATION SKILLS

Communication skills are tools which enable a child to express his needs and to establish healthy relationships with persons in his environment. A child uses these skills to gather information about himself and to establish his identity in the world. In examining literature relevant to communication, Eagle (1982) defined communication skills as tools "needed by an individual to understand his surroundings, to express his responses, and to use spoken language functionally" (p. 21). While the desire to communicate may be intrinsically motivated, functional skills must be learned through imitation and experimentation.

The severely visually impaired child communicates in a manner more similar than dissimilar to that of his sighted peers. He must (a) decode, (b) encode, and (c) send information in order to interact with his environment. In other words, he receives information, interprets it, and expresses himself in observable ways (Ross, 1980). While all children communicate in this manner, the visually disabled child may lack sensory information which inhibits his ability to perceive and respond to incoming stimuli. Figure 4 illustrates the process through which the handicapped child interacts with his environment.

FIGURE 4
Conceptual Model of the Communication Process

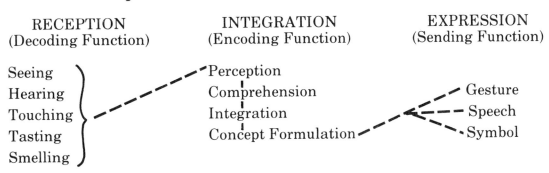

RECEPTION (Decoding Function)	INTEGRATION (Encoding Function)	EXPRESSION (Sending Function)

Seeing
Hearing
Touching
Tasting
Smelling

Perception
Comprehension
Integration
Concept Formulation

Gesture
Speech
Symbol

As illustrated, the child with normal or near normal vision receives information through all of his senses, but he relies most heavily upon his visual sense. He requires multiple experiences with objects and ideas in order to demonstrate conceptual understanding, but with exposure and direction, he develops a systematic and jointed view of things. The sighted child explores the world by reaching for objects and experiences outside of himself. He actively imitates and manipulates his environment. His gestural, spoken, and symbolic response patterns are limited only by his experience and imagination.

In comparison, the visually disabled child "collects" information through any remaining vision and through more deliberate use of his other senses. He does not develop a "sixth sense," as is occasionally suggested, but rather, he refines uses of existing senses. The blind child relies upon tactile manipulation and "muscle sense," that is, sequential movement, to acquire knowledge. He requires multiple exposure to objects and ideas to achieve conceptual understanding, as does the visually capable child; but he may never achieve understanding of many concepts due to the difficulty of exploration or abstractness of concept. The visually impaired child may not reach out for new experiences, but instead, may wait for them to "happen" to him. He is limited in his ability to imitate visually modeled behavior, and he may not manipulate objects unless encouraged by others to do so. The gestural, spoken, and symbolic responses with which this child expresses himself are frequently affected by an inability to learn through visual modeling or by restricted life experience. The visually disabled child must be challenged by significant others to communicate.

Cognitive Function: The Concept of Wholeness

The visually disabled child may not grasp the gestalt, or circumscribed whole, of a given concept. This is especially true in the case of those with congenital blindness. To compensate for a lack of information, the music therapist must provide the child with repeated exposure to objects or events. This will enable the child to achieve maximum understanding. His ability to extract information from experiences, and then to formulate more generalized concepts from them, has a direct effect upon his ability to communicate effectively with others and engage in subsequent learning. The following tale illustrates the difficulty a visually disabled child might have in perceiving a "whole" concept as "the sum of its parts." In the story of the "Blind Men and the Elephant," a number of blind men each explored different portions of the elephant's anatomy and then reported their conceptualizations of "elephant." Each man accurately described that part of the elephant which he had experienced as his understanding of "elephant" as a whole. Still, none approached an accurate definition of the whole concept. The story conveys an experience not uncommon to the congenitally blind child. To prevent this faulty integration of information, the therapist must teach concepts through multi-sensory, concrete instructional experiences. To achieve integration, the "blind man" must tactually explore the elephant while the animal sleeps, eats, bathes, kneels, walks, and stands still. He must listen to the elephant, smell the elephant, read about it, and listen to the observations of others to gain his most accurate understanding of the creature. The blind child will learn most effectively through participation in a well-planned, concrete, multi-sensory program which provides "hands on" experience and frequent evaluation of learning by the therapist.

The manner in which a severely visually impaired child derives knowledge about his environment is, of course, affected by his disability. Vision is a unifying sense which allows the individual to organize sensory stimuli into concepts which comprise his view of the world. Distorted vision or lack of vision limits exploration so that the child may explore only one object at a time. Therefore, simultaneous comparisons between objects is difficult. The disabled child cannot accurately explore extremely small objects, therefore, he must find or be offered other means of exposure to this information. Because he is limited in his understanding of distant objects, his perceptual grasp of the sky, moon, and stars is extremely distorted. He learns little from fragile objects; his tactile exploration of an insect often destroys the creature, leaving the child frustrated and without understanding. Objects which are displayed behind glass prohibit the blind child from any exploration and provide the partially seeing child with an image distorted by reflections in the glass. Some objects remain too dangerous to explore. A sighted child can perceive a rhinocerous in a zoo although he is unable to touch the animal; the severely visually impaired child receives little or no visual information about the animal and must rely upon data gained from models which lack accuracy and promote conceptual distortion. The blind child is limited in his understanding of fast moving objects because he is unable to effectively explore them visually or tactually as they function. The child must formulate a concept of "motor" by touching external parts on an inoperative machine; he may perceive the motor as a large, unmoving object comprised only of its external parts. He must rely upon second-hand information concerning its function. Within these limitations, the therapist serves as a facilitator and teacher, to promote the relationship of child to environment.

Communications with the Child: Implications for Therapy

The music therapist need not be visually disabled to work effectively with visually impaired children. However, the sighted therapist must learn as much as possible about how his clients view the world in order to develop appropriate teaching techniques. The music therapist must learn to describe objects in terms of shape, texture, and location of objects in a given space, rather than by visual descriptors. The use of some sighted terms should be avoided; phrases such as "over there" or "over here" are ineffective in providing direction. The therapist should, instead, give directions in relation to the familiar: "The tambourine is located on the floor to your right about one step." Note that the direction was given beginning with the most general direction (on the floor) and ending with the most specific direction (to your right about one step). This enables the child to search for the object in a logical progressive fashion. Directions also can be given using some familiar object in the room as a reference point, as in: "The drum is lying on the table just to the right of the door. It is located on the front left corner of the table as you face it."

In most cases, the therapist should not avoid the use of "sighted terms" when conversing with severely impaired or even blind children. An exception might be when giving directions which incorporate color to a child to whom a "color descriptor" carries no meaning. In general, "sighted terms," such as "see," "blind," or "red," are words which the child will hear and must accept as an element of the vision-oriented world of which he is a part. It is difficult for a sighted person to avoid these terms and doing so, more often than not, indicates to the visually impaired person the speaker's discomfort with the disability. A more desirable strategy would be to address visual concepts, such as color, in nonvisual terms. For example, a therapist when asked about specific colors might describe them in terms of feelings, such as: "Orange is a warm color, hot like the sun, and loud. Blue in a cool color, like water in a summer pond, and soft. Sometimes people say they are 'blue,' meaning they are sad." Color can never be fully understood by the congenitally blind child, but it should be discussed on demand. The partially sighted child wants exposure to color. It should be made available to him whenever possible. The music therapist will communicate effectively with the blind child regardless of developed skills, if he approaches the child with respect, kindness, patience, and consistency.

The therapist should be mindful of the following points in reference to communication:

(a) The therapist should identify himself when entering a room where a blind child is alone. He might say "Hi, it's Ms. Smith," so the child will always know the identity and location of the person in the room. In time, the therapist's voice should become familiar so that verification becomes unnecessary.

(b) The therapist should indicate when he is leaving the presence of the blind child so that the child is not left "talking to himself." A simple, "I'm going now" or "I'll see you later" will generally suffice.

(c) The therapist should always talk directly to the blind child rather than through a third person and he should encourage others to do the same. Generally, an intermediary is not necessary to facilitate a conversation. If an individual attempts to speak to the child through the therapist, the conversation should be directed to the child. A nod in the direction of the blind child will serve the purpose. The child should speak for himself whenever possible.

(d) The therapist should avoid private conversation with a third party in the presence of the blind child. The use of hand signals in this situation is not the most effective means of communication. If it is necessary to converse privately with the third party, the therapist should excuse himself from the presence of the child.

(e) When talking with a blind child, the therapist should speak in a "normal" tone of voice. It is not necessary to speak in an unusually loud voice. Lack of vision does not impair hearing. This is a common mistake.

(f) When conversing with a blind child, the therapist should focus his attention on the child. The therapist who moves around the room or shuffles instruments when talking or listening is not an attentive conversation partner.

(g) The therapist should be sensitive to the increased needs of the blind child in group situations. The visually limited child cannot accurately assess group dynamics, as he is ineffective in interpreting physical gestures. The therapist should facilitate successful group interaction by sensitive observation of individual and group needs.

(h) When introducing a blind or severely visually disabled person to persons in a group, it is occasionally appropriate to physically "situate" some children in places to promote successful socialization. The therapist may need to initiate conversation when approaching a group with a blind child. This may stimulate recognition of group members by the approaching child. A simple, "Hi Mary, how are you?" cues recognition.

Teaching Communication Skills

When teaching communication skills to severely visually impaired children, the therapist should (a) use a vocabulary sensitive to the child's sensory experience while not avoiding common "sighted terms," (b) consider the limitations of learning imposed by the disability and teach techniques which will enable him to compensate for his limitations, (c) consider the child's strengths and reinforce them, (d) individualize learning materials and instruction techniques when possible, (e) teach the child to use equipment designed for use by the visually handicapped, (f) structure frequent, multi-sensory exploration of environmental objects, sometimes for extended period of time, (g) provide constant activity-appropriate sensory stimulation to maintain attending skills, (h) give ability-appropriate directions—for example, progress from one-step to two-step directions only when the child's readiness level dictates, and (i) listen to the child because he can sometimes accurately assess his own needs and direct therapist-effective teaching techniques.

Sensory Perceptual Skills

The visually disabled child interacts with his environment by receiving information through his senses, formulating concepts, and responding to external stimuli. Sometimes, however, he experiences difficulty in processing information received through one or more of these channels. The music therapist has proven an effective teacher in developing related skills. Appendix B provides a skeletal outline of basic skills for use in planning music therapy activities. The therapist also should consider the following goals[3] as suggestions for treatment and make necessary modifications to meet the child's needs.

Sensory Perceptual Skills: Auditory Stimulation

The child will:

(a) respond to environmental sounds of markedly different dynamic levels.

(b) respond to human vocalization.

(c) respond to the sound of his own voice.

(d) anticipate sounds.

(e) locate the sound of a musical instrument by pointing to the source of the sound.

(f) locate the sound of a musical instrument by moving toward the source of the sound.

(g) physically track the sound source as it moves in the room.

(h) demonstrate ear-hand and residual eye-hand coordination by grasping a sounding object.

(i) discriminate between two sounds by indicating sameness or difference.

(j) group instruments according to like and unlike properties.

(k) discriminate sameness or difference in sounds using high and low pitches.

(l) discriminate sameness or difference in sounds using loud and soft instrumental sounds (same instrument, different instruments).

(m) match two rhythmic patterns of the same tempo when presented with three rhythmic patterns.

(n) group instruments by like and unlike shapes, sizes, and sounds.

(o) match two instrumental sounds of like timbre when presented with three musical sounds.

(p) imitate clapped rhythmic patterns of increasing length and complexity.

(q) imitate rhythmic patterns of increasing length and complexity played on different "body instruments" (snap fingers, clap hands, pat knees, stamp feet) and discriminate "snapped" from "clapped" patterns.

(r) vocally imitate tonal patterns of increasing length and complexity on one or more instruments.

Sensory Perceptual Skills: Visual Stimulation

The child will:

(a) turn his head (eyes) toward a light source such as a penlight with colored opaque paper at the end of it.

(b) visually fixate on an object (such as a tambourine with a light behind it).

(c) visually track lighted object in vertical, then horizontal direction.

(d) visually track an unlighted object in a vertical, then a horizontal direction.

(e) turn his head and body to continue tracking an object outside his immediate visual field.

(f) visually track an object to the point of disappearance, and then search for the object. (This demonstrates an awareness of object permanence.)

(g) demonstrate eye-hand coordination by reaching for and grasping a stationary, then a moving instrument.

(h) visually search for a fallen instrument until he locates it.

(i) visually discriminate between objects of two or more different colors.

(j) visually discriminate between two or more objects of identical shape, but of different size.

(k) visually discriminate between two or more objects of different texture (rough appearance, smooth appearance).

(l) match actual instruments to pictures of the instruments.

(m) visually locate pictures of specified objects (instruments) among objects in a drawing (demonstrates figure-ground discrimination).

(n) recognize an object by looking at its parts.

(o) recognize an object from a variety of visual angles.

Sensory Perceptual Skills: Tactile Stimulation

The child will:

(a) identify various textures and temperatures.

(b) examine objects willingly by touch.

(c) identify objects by tactile exploration.

(d) initiate and maintain contact with vibrating objects.

(e) discriminate among two or more objects of different texture.

(f) describe an object by feeling it.

(g) discriminate hard objects from soft objects.

(h) discriminate among objects of varying temperatures (including gradations of hot and cold).

(i) discriminate among instruments and other objects of varying size and shape.

(j) tactually discriminate among the vibrations radiated from varying musical objects.

(k) group objects of like shape and/or texture.

(l) discriminate loud from soft, near from distant, vibrations.

(m) imitate rhythmic patterns on one or more musical instrument(s).

Sensory Perceptual Skills: Olfactory Stimulation

The child will:

(a) demonstrate awareness of smell by facial expression, turning toward or away from strongly scented stimuli, pleasantly scented stimuli or unpleasantly scented stimuli presented to the nasal area.

(b) discriminate among two or more pleasant or unpleasant smells presented in the nasal region.

(c) discriminate among two or more pleasant or unpleasant smells presented at increasing distances from the child.

(d) identify the source of common smells.

(e) describe a substance by smell.

Sensory Perceptual Skills: Gustatory Stimulation

The child will:

(a) respond by changing facial expression, changing tongue movements, or turning toward or away from sweet, sour, salty, or bitter tasting food placed on tongue or lip area.

(b) identify food by taste.

(c) discriminate among sweet, sour, salty, and bitter tasting foods.

(d) discriminate, by taste, among foods which look alike (granulated sugar, salt, etc.)

(e) describe foods by their textures and desired temperatures.

DEVELOPMENT OF ACADEMIC SKILLS

Eagle (1982) operationally defined academic skills as "all the techniques used by an individual to learn and comprehend knowledge" (p. 25). For the purpose of discussion, these skills will include sensorimotor, pre-number, and pre-reading skills in addition to traditionally defined academic skills.

Play activities can stimulate physical, emotional, and academic skill development. Research by Lowenfeld (1973) indicates that a child develops as much during the first 4 years of life as in the next 13 years of life. Because play activities are the child's primary means for acquiring knowledge, infant stimulation games should be provided to promote (a) the formation of strong primary human attachments, (b) interest in environmental objects, and (c) physical strength, coordination, and mobility. The learning of sensorimotor, pre-number, pre-reading, and early social skills may be encouraged by parent-initiated home stimulation and formal infant stimulation programs. Preschool enrichment programs for older children may also contribute to later educational success.

The visually impaired child, like the nondisabled child, relies heavily upon early life experiences to provide a foundation for successful academic development (Lowenfeld, 1973). While early stimulation is vital to preschool preparation, many parents of blind children fail to implement these necessary games. Instead, many parents overprotect or even neglect their child as a result of grief or guilt felt in birthing a handicapped human being. So, many of these children may require extensive training in formal readiness programs to prepare them for school placement (Meyen, 1978). Developmental delay in infancy often assures delay in later stages of development, while success in early learning provides a foundation to enable future academic success.

An understanding of cognitive development is necessary to the planning and implementation of music therapy activities for academic skill development. Piaget's theory of intellectual development serves as a desirable model for this purpose; his theories about learning provide insight into the sequencing of activities to promote cognitive growth.

According to Piaget, the stages of cognitive development are: (1) the sensorimotor, (2) pre-operational, (3) the concrete operational, and (4) the formal operations. Piaget describes each developmental stage by indicating characteristic thought processes and the approximate chronological age of the nondisabled child at each progressive stage of development. It should be noted that, because of his sensory and experiential disadvantage, the blind child of average intelligence is frequently two or more years older at any academic grade level, and probably within each developmental stage, than the sighted child with equivalent intelligence (Lowenfeld, 1973). Music goals and activities developed for use in each growth stage should consider the readiness level and cognitive ability of the child.

Piaget: The Sensorimotor Stage

According to Piaget, the sensorimotor stage of development spans the first two years of life for the sighted child of average abilities. During these years, infant response progressses from chance reflexive reaction to stimuli, to more deliberate, patterned response. The child learns to manipulate objects within his immediate environment and gains a sense of "object permanence." He will search for a toy removed from his sight rather than accept its disappearance. He learns to repeat behavior patterns which will result in need fulfillment. For example, he will cry until he is held, fed, or changed according to his needs. The sighted child also learns to imitate simple actions of others (Lowenfeld, 1973). Visual disability may limit the development of healthy patterned response to environmental stimuli. It may impede interest and exploratory action. Visual disorder will delay imitative behavior and sensory integration. During this stage, the child should experiment with all his senses. He should be encouraged to use any residual vision by exposure to color, shape, and texture. Interest in tactile exploration of temperature, texture, shape, and size should be rewarded. Experiences should be provided which encourage sensory integration; for example, objects should be adapted to encourage additional stimulation. A bell added to the ear of a stuffed bear and pleasing perfume added to the fabric might enhance interest, add to familiarity of the object, and help the child find the bear when dropped.

The partially sighted child should learn to track visual and auditory stimuli. Many activities encourage tracking. For example, a penlight with various colored tips moved across the child's visual field may generate interest and encourage visual tracking, as does a simple rhythm instrument similarly used. In addition, the sound of the instrument encourages localization and identification of sound. Rattles and bells are excellent instruments for tracking.

Piaget: The Pre-operational Stage

The pre-operational stage of development encompasses the second through fourth years of life. Two components of this stage are: (a) the symbolic and (b) the intuitive thought phases. The symbolic, or preconceptual, level of development is entered at about age 2. Behavior imitated in previous years is internalized in this stage; that is, it acquires meaning and symbolic representation. In play, manipulation of objects becomes a game of "make believe," wherein the child acts out observed behavior. He begins to comprehend language symbolic of familiar objects, and he refers to some objects by name. He requests objects outside his immediate view and talks about previously experienced events. The child should be encouraged to play with common objects in his environment, including objects of various shapes, textures, weights, sizes, and sounds. As the child's motor and perceptual skills develop, he should be encouraged to play in substances of texture, such as water, sand, and soap. Food substances, such as flour, peanut butter, and fruit, might be felt; he might smell food and also taste it for increased pleasure! As his mobility increases, the sighted child moves greater distances to explore his environment. The blind child, however, must be strongly encouraged to do so. Materials appropriate for play at this time include colorful hanging objects and beads, bright flashing lights, bells on shoes and on a string, wind chimes, warm and cool objects (for comparison) as well as knobs, zippers, latches, plastic balls, and spoons. Other materials include drums, rattles, wooden beads, sponges of all sizes and shapes, large wooden blocks and light plastic blocks, an elastic band hung with bracelets, blocks with bells inside, and safe vibrating objects of all types. Other play materials are plastic containers filled with objects that sound, keys, a busy box filled with string, spools, locks, play dough, food stuffs, rocking chairs, rubber and "nerf" balls, and milk cartons filled with beans (Klebanoff, 1973).

The child enters the intuitive thought stage of the pre-operational level of development at about 4 years of age. He continues to exhibit characteristic behavior through approximately his seventh year. During this time, language becomes repetitive and verbalization occurs as a monologue. The child seems egocentric but will interact meaningfully with others to share information. He imitates modeled behavior to learn desired skills and expands his social contacts to include persons outside his nuclear family. He shows interest in manipulating the world around him (Lowenfeld, 1973). In terms of the developmental therapy model, the child should be encouraged to "respond to the environment with pleasure." He should experience (a) appropriate body contact and touch, (b) consistency in routine with room for exploration of interest-catching objects and events, and (c) answers to his questions.

Structured music activities should include exploration of sound and movement, alone and in the company of others. The child should be encouraged to play instruments and to dance, to observe and imitate modeled behavior. The therapist should provide exposure to rhythm instruments, recordings of familiar sounds, improvised music, and stories to encourage exploration. Fingerplays should be introduced if the child's visual functioning permits. These activities encourage imitation and fine motor development. Singing activities which involve action and the presentation of nonmusical or musical information should be widely used at this level. Pitched and unpitched instruments should be incorporated into individual and group activity. Pitched Orff instruments may be used with low-vision children if well marked visually (in black or white) to enable discrimination among tone bars. Lighting must be appropriate for each child and extensive exposure to these instruments is necessary to promote successful structured play. Resources which include creative sensory stimulation activities for young children include, *Home Stimulation for the Young Developmentally Disabled Child* (Klebanoff, 1973), and *Activity-Centered Learning in the Home: Workjobs for Parents* (Baratta-Lorton, 1975).

Piaget: The Concrete Operational Stage

The concrete operational stage spans the child's seventh year through the time when he becomes capable of consistent concrete problem-solving. During these years, the child develops an ability to think systematically, and to relate his experience to an organized whole or gestalt. Analytically, his reasoning progresses from an inductive to a deductive system of reasoning. During this stage, the child becomes able to establish systems of classification. He can classify objects according to similar and dissimilar traits and can manipulate symbols, such as words and numbers. He communicates functionally through language, but often uses words without a clear understanding of meaning. During these years, the child actively seeks to imitate the behavior of persons outside of his immediate family.

The visually disabled child generally experiences delay at this stage of development. Difficulty in reasoning, classifying, understanding verbal meaning, and learning desirable social skills by imitation are the direct result of lack of experience, due to visual disability. Lack of adequate vision affects interaction with one's environment by distorting receptive, integrative and expressive communicative processes (see also, section on Development of Communication Skills). Therefore, cognitive functions are inhibited. When compared to sighted children of equal cognitive ability, the blind child functions approximately two years below age level (Lowenfeld, 1973). Music activities in the concrete operational stage should include active and passive listening activities, vocal and instrumental music-making, and movement to music. Because the child seeks the companionship of others, participation in musical groups is appropriate. Group interaction provides the child with feedback from group members and encourages him to subdue expression of personal needs for the sake of the group. Group participation provides an arena for learning and practice of social skills. The severely visually impaired child should participate in music activities with normally sighted children whenever possible. The visually impaired child generally can function musically on a level equal to his peers.

Piaget: The Formal Operation Stage

The child enters the fourth, and final, period of cognitive development at about eleven years of age. The formal operations stage is characterized by the demonstration of abstract as well as concrete reasoning ability. The adolescent is able to formulate ideas in the form of hypotheses to be tested through deductive reasoning, and to use language to communicate effectively. The visually handicapped youth may demonstrate difficulty in understanding cause-and-effect relationships—that is, A caused B to occur—and may have difficulty expressing ideas in abstract terms. Music activities should continue to promote self-esteem, communication skills, and music learning for pleasure. Because visually handicapped adolescents identify with music in much the same way as their sighted peers, music activity can be used as a bridge to facilitate communication between these groups. Appropriate activities include music listening, lyric discussion, and guitar playing in groups.

Use of Braille Music

The Braille Music Code was developed for use in teaching vocal and instrumental music to braille readers. While it is a useful tool in many instances, braille music should not be taught to all students. Rather, it should be used only if the braille readers demonstrate an established command of necessary academic codes. Braille is a difficult system of symbols which comprises math, science, and music codes, in addition to the literary code. The therapist should determine if a student's musical goals warrant the learning of an additional code. If not, note learning or another modified system can be used for instruction. A student who learns the Braille Music Code without first mastering previously introduced codes may experience reading difficulty and experience confusion when reading in all codes. He may suffer reading reversals or missed symbols, as the same six-dot braille cell serves as the building block in each code. Teaching the Braille Music Code before the child is academically ready may frustrate success rather than structure it.

The music therapist may expect limited access to music notated in braille. A limited selection of braille music is available through the American Printing House for the Blind; some private parties sometimes provide braille music on demand. However, the therapist who uses this code must usually braille his own music.

Music in large print is more readily available than braille music. Music in standard print sizes may be enlarged by special duplicating machines often located in schools serving severely visually impaired children. (Print enlargement achieved through duplication is lawful within limits when used for instructional purposes.) Some print readers can read music as written in the large print editions of established instrumental instruction series. Braille readers should not be taught to read printed music reproduced in relief or raised print, as symbols used in standard notation are not comparable to the Braille Code. Adventitiously blinded students generally do not possess the tactile sensitivity to read raised print and, therefore, fail in the attempt. (For further information concerning reproduction of music in large print or braille, contact the American Printing House for the Blind in Louisville, Kentucky.)

A common myth exists that blind persons as a group are more musically talented than sighted persons; however, research does not support this thesis. Blind children do not possess a sixth "musical" sense, nor are they "gifted as compensation for blindness" as many believe. Rather visually impaired persons refine their use of remaining senses in the absence of a primary sense to promote the development of auditory and tactile senses, and to facilitate the integration of sensory stimuli. Blind children in residential schools have traditionally received early music instruction. Some of these children have excelled in music as a result of their training and practice. Therefore, if blind persons seem to excel in music, it is because early exposure and hard work have resulted in the development of musical skill. If sighted children were "equally saturated with music," more of them might demonstrate "musical talent" (Lowenfield, 1973).

Teaching Academic Skills

When teaching pre-academic and academic skills to severely visually impaired children, the music therapist should (a) collect information from records and personnel to determine current levels of academic functioning, (b) maintain close communication with special educators so as to reinforce behavior desired of the child, (c) consider the child's strengths and reinforce these strengths, (d) consider the limitations of learning imposed by the child's disability and develop techniques compatible with those used in the classroom to allow the child to compensate as much as possible for his limitations, (e) function as support personnel under the guidance of the primary teacher, (f) utilize professional resources with the immediate facility and beyond, and (g) seek additional training in techniques useful in teaching severely visually impaired children. The music therapist has proven effective in prompting pre-academic skills, such as (a) motor readiness skills, (b) concept development, and (c) reading readiness skills. While an effective teacher, the music therapist is not a "jack-of-all trades"; he should, therefore, be mindful of his weaknesses as well as his strengths in teaching academics.

DEVELOPMENT OF MOTOR SKILLS

Motor skills are operationally defined as those skills which facilitate body awareness through integration of (a) sensorimotor stimuli, (b) "gross," or large muscle movement, and (c) "fine," or small muscle movement. Motor development involves refinement of (1) "nonlocomotor" movement, that is, movement within the child's personal space, and (2) "locomotor" movement, that is, movement from the child's present to his desired position in space. Movement is physical action: "It involves space, is concerned with skills and body actions and takes place in relation to objects and other people" (Kratz, 1977, p. 3). Movement provides a means of reducing tension experienced in response to stress (Knight, 1972). To the visually limited child, movement is stimulation, self-protection, and play, a tool for learning and a means of self-expression.

The visually limited child progresses through a pattern of physical development not unlike that of his sighted peers. However, he often matures at a slower rate. Physical development proceeds in a head-to-foot direction and from a pre-walking to a walking stage. In preparation for movement through space, a toddler learns to posture himself for balance. He begins by holding his head up. He then sits, stands, crawls, and finally walks. The blind child is deprived of visual information which teaches posture and effective locomotor movement. As a result, he appears clumsy and motorically inefficient. Balance and body alignment affected, his movement through space appears defensive and unsure. His movement lacks fluidity and spontaneity. His gait is shuffled and his muscles seem stiff. He moves as if his body is a burden to be carried, a prison without escape. Physical development is not directly retarded by his lack of vision, but it is influenced by this condition. Opportunities for locomotor movement may be restricted by the parent who overprotects, neglects, or misinterprets his child's needs. The child may lack strength or coordination because he remains relatively immobile. He fails to move toward unfamiliar or unseen objects at a distance due to lack of awareness or fear of movement (Lowenfield, 1973).

Movement facilitates learning by enabling exploration. Restricted mobility directly affects the blind child's ability to function academically. According to Kratz (1977), the blind child

> has the same need for muscular activity (as the sighted child). His emotional characteristics, his need for mastering his environment and self are no different from those of anyone else, except in terms of intensity. Thus those about him, who function in this environment and exert influence upon him, must be aware of the vital part that movement must play with regard to both his physical development and his development of what we call the "self." The need for movement and activity is heightened in all of its dimensions when one sensory avenue, in this case, sight, has been impaired. Without movement, the blind child's world is limited by the reach of his arms . . . (p.3).

Music activity can be used to promote motor learning in both the pre-walking stage and the walking stage. *Pre-walking* skills involve simple nonlocomotor movements such as elevation of head, sitting, and standing. The *walking* stage incorporates refined gross and fine motor coordination, and movement through space. In addition, concepts, such as body image, directionality, and laterality, and put to use.

The average sighted child enters the pre-walking stage at about 16 weeks of age. A behavior characteristic of this stage is the ability to visually track a moving object, and to reach for it. This child enters the walking stage at about 15 months of age, at which time he stands, balances, and moves forward on his own. He later runs, skips, hops, and dances. The blind child experiences developmental delay in both growth periods (Lowenfield, 1973). (See the sections on Development of Communication Skills and Development of Academic Skills, for a discussion of sensory stimulation in the pre-walking period of development.)

Relaxation

Severely visually impaired children are frequently tense because they lack vision to guide free movement in and through space. Ironically, these children rely heavily upon "muscle sense" to learn. The blind child learns to tie his shoe through a sequential pattern of movements. He learns mobility skills by practicing a series of deliberate muscle responses. It is essential that the music therapist teach the child to relax in order to increase his effective use of this "muscle sense."

Simple music activities can teach deep breathing and help to develop an awareness of tense versus relaxed muscles. Slow rhythmic breathing in various body positions may be taught by the therapist, first without music to encourage the focusing of attention on breathing and "muscle sense," and later with music as background for relaxation activities. The therapist should be careful not to introduce too much in the way of external stimuli at one time. Many "self-awareness" activities are best taught initially without music as background. Silence allows the child to focus intensely upon himself in the initial stage of relaxation. Later, a specific musical selection may be paired with relaxation training and serve as a cue to prompt this response. Music might also accompany exercises to (a) encourage relaxation of the child's extremities and trunk, (b) increase joint flexibility, especially in the spine and chest, (c) reduce the rigidity of specific muscles, and (d) improve posture and fluidity of movement within personal space or in movement through space. A consistently tense child does not move efficiently nor does he play or learn with ease. Additional suggestions for relaxation techniques can be found in "The Role of Relaxation" in *Movement Without Sight: Physical Activity and Dance for the Visually Handicapped* (Kratz, 1977), and the chapters, "Movement" and "Blind/Visually Impaired" in *Alike and Different: The Clinical and Educational Use of Orff-Schulwerk* (Bitcon, 1976). *You Must Relax* (Jacobson, 1970) relates established relaxation techniques that can be adapted for use with visually impaired clients.

Body Image

Body image involves cognitive and physical integration of information concerning his body mass. The child learns about his body by experiencing (a) awareness of his body as a unit—understanding its size, strengths, weaknesses, and appearances, (b) his body in relation to objects in space, (c) his body in relation to other persons and their perception of him, and (d) his awareness of direction in space. One's body image constantly changes as physical changes occur and additional knowledge is acquired (Vise, 1972).

The visually disabled child should learn body concepts in sequence. According to Vise (1972), a desirable strategy is to teach the (a) body parts of the learner, (b) body surfaces of the learner, (c) body parts and surfaces on the person himself, (d) body parts and surfaces in relation to another person when the learner is standing behind that person, and then (e) body parts and surfaces in relation to another person when the child is facing that person. Songs, such as "Head, Shoulders, Knees, and Toes" (Birkenshaw, 1977) and "Touch" from the Hap Palmer record album, *Getting to Know Myself* are examples of the many songs which teach body concepts using music as a "physical structure for learning activity" (Duerkson, 1978).

Learning of personal body surfaces, specifically includes recognition of the following body planes: "front of body, side of body, back of body, stomach, back, turning whole body against a wall, sliding hand down either an arm or leg, both outside and inside, sliding hand down sides, sliding feet on floor, and turning whole body on floor (leg roll)" (Vise, 1972, p. 32). Body surfaces might be taught through song in much the same way music is used to teach body parts. A given song might direct the movement of a tambourine up or down the front or side plane of the body. Other lyrics might direct the child to "show the *bottom* of his foot." Some actions require the movement of a body part to a position parallel with a structural (external) surface; for example, when directed, the child must "turn his *front* to the wall" or "turn his *left side* to the wall." Music as background in such activities should be used selectively. When used prematurely, the music may attract the child's attention away from the "muscle sense" he uses to learn these concepts. Music should be used only when the child has demonstrated a basic understanding of body-surface concepts. When it is used, music can encourage movement. A blind child who moves too deliberately might learn to relax and demonstrate more "fluid" movement to pleasing music.

Songs and simple dance routines can be devised to teach body parts and surfaces in relation to another person. According to Vise (1972), the therapist must teach the location of body parts and surfaces on a person standing *behind* the child, and later, standing in front and *facing* the child. For example, the verbal command "touch your right hand to my right hip" would be executed by the child as the therapist stands *behind* and later, *faces* the child.

Orientation and Mobility

Orientation and mobility refer to the competencies which enable the severely visually impaired person to achieve safe, efficient, and fluid movement through his environment. *Orientation* involves utilization of a person's sensory processes to establish his position in relation to significant objects in his environment. *Mobility* is the actual locomotion of that person from his present position in space to his desired position in space. Orientation and mobility skills are a primary concern to the severely visually impaired child as his success in these areas influences (a) his self-image, (b) his perception of his environment via his successful exploratory experience, (c) his performance of important social roles, and (d) society's judgment of him (Coker & Dhindsa, 1979; Lowenfield, 1973).

Peripathologists, or "mobility instructors," are special educators who teach orientation and mobility skills to totally blind persons and partially sighted persons in need of these services. (See the section on Eye Care and Other Vision Specialists.) The music therapist should teach basic orientation skills, and is, in fact, well-trained to do that. However, he should work closely with the peripathologist. The following perceptual and motor skills can be taught through music therapy activities:

Pattern Walking
1. Walking forward and backward.
2. Walking to the left and to the right.
3. Walking forward, backward, to the left, and to the right in various combinations.
4. Walking previously presented patterns but instead walking diagonally.

Describing Circles
1. Describing circles with the hands on the floor, moving forward (toward the body), backward (away from the body), to the left, and to the right.
2. Describing circles with the arms (movement is both parallel and perpendicular to the body).
3. Describing circles with the feet and legs (movement is to the left and to the right, and the person is standing in place).
4. Describing the circumference of a circle when the person is facing the center of the circle (so that movement is to the left or to the right).
5. Describing the circumference of a circle when the person has his side toward the center of the circle (so that movement around the circle is either clockwise or counterclockwise).
6. Describing the form of a figure eight.

Turning in Place
1. Turning a full circle with the child as the center of a group.
2. Turning a half circle with the child as the center of a group.
3. Turning a quarter turn with the child as the center of a group.
4. Turning a three-quarter turn with the child as the center of a group.
5. Turning a full circle with the child using only orientation cues of a structural or auditory nature.
6. Turning a half circle with the child using only orientation cues of a structural or auditory nature.
7. Turning a quarter turn with the child using only orientation of a structural nature.

Locomotor and Non-Locomotor Movement
1. Walking.
2. Running.
3. Jumping in place.
4. Hopping in place.
5. Dancing an "Indian dance movement" as a preliminary lead-up activity for skipping.
6. Walking the "sore toe" walk as a preliminary lead up activity for galloping (toes up).
7. Walking lightly to a waltz rhythm moving forward and in a circle.
8. Walking like an elephant, sliding like a "skater," and imitating vehicles to provide variation in walking patterns.
9. Walking on tip toes in forward, backward, and in a circular direction.
10. Walking on heels forward, backward, and in a circle.
11. Jumping forward, backward, and in a circular direction.
12. Walking backward in a circle.
13. Galloping forward and in a circular direction.
14. Skipping forward and in a circular direction, and in a circle.

Stretching Exercises
1. Stretching the upper body while sitting on the floor (alternately straightening and curving the spinal column).
2. Stretching the feet and legs while sitting on the floor:
    a. pointing the feet,
    b. flexing the feet, stretching the entire body,
    c. stretching upward,
    d. stretching downward,
    e. arching the body forward,
    f. arching the body backward.
3. Stretching the upper body while standing:
    a. twisting the upper body,
    b. tilting the upper body,
    c. stretching the spinal column.
4. Stretching the arms:
    a. moving parallel to the body,
    b. moving perpendicular to the body,
    c. moving parallel and perpendicular to the body.
5. Stretching the legs:
    a. swinging the legs forward, backward, and to the side with the raised foot pointed,
    b. swinging the legs forward, backward, and to the side with the raised foot flexed,
    c. describing circles with the toes when the supporting leg is straight,
    d. describing circles with the toes when the supporting leg is bent.

Balancing
1. Executing a "tight rope walk" moving forward and backward.
2. Executing a "tight rope walk" in a circle moving in clockwise and counterclockwise directions.
3. Walking in half circles moving forward.
4. Walking in half circles moving clockwise and counterclockwise in a circle (Vise, 1972, pp. 31-34).

   Movement activities should be introduced in their simplest form, and should be directed by specific physical, structural, and/or aural cues. A physical cue might be as supportive as sitting or standing behind the child and moving him through an action, or a minimal touch cue. Physical cues, such as those involving whole body support, serve as structural cues as they limit the child's space; many blind children require structural cues for movement. Surfaces such as walls and floors are useful for the sake of orientation. When using structural support surfaces, activities which allow the child to remain in constant contact with the wall or floor should sequentially precede those during which structural contact is removed. For example, a child might learn to walk in *forward* and *backward* directions while touching a wall with the hand nearest that surface. When ready, he may be required to repeat the movement at a distance one or two steps (feet) from the wall. Sequentially, he should practice walking prior to hopping or skipping because walking provides constant contact (left or right foot) with the floor. Auditory cues include verbal direction and many nonverbal sound cues, which can structure movement. For example, repeated rhythms may cue walking, jumping, or skipping responses. A rhythmic cue played on one instrument may cue forward movement and another, backward movement. Sound cues can be generated from various locations in a room and can structure location and identification of sound stimuli. A child might practice localizing sound in an activity which requires that he turn or move toward one or more instruments played individually from separate areas of a room. If asked to name the source of the stimuli, he learns to identify sound. Physical, structural, and auditory cues are useful in structuring learning experiences; these cues may be paired or extinguished as necessary to promote effective movement. Activities for use in the promotion of sensorimotor skills at the kindergarten and primary levels are available through the book, *Daily Sensorimotor Training Activities: A Handbook for Teachers and Parents of Preschool Children* (Braley, Konicki & Leedy, 1968). *Orientation and Mobility to the Primary Grades Taught Through the Media of Rhythms, Dance Exercises and Body Movement Exercises* (Vise, 1972) serves as an excellent resource manual for use by music therapists.

Sighted Guide Techniques

   A *sighted guide* is a person who accompanies a blind person in a travel situation so that faster and more efficient locomotion can be accomplished by the visually impaired individual. It is imperative that the music therapist be able to demonstrate these skills before he adapts them for use with severely/profoundly handicapped persons and/or small children. To this end, the following sighted guide techniques are not difficult to learn. However, practice is required if these procedures are to become useful techniques.

   (a) Establish contact with the blind person by maneuvering *your left arm* into contact with *his right hand.* (He might prefer to take your right arm with his left hand.) The blind person should grasp your arm just above the elbow so that his thumb rests on the outside and fingers on the inside of your arm nearest your body. This places his forearm parallel to the ground and his upper arm parallel and close to his body. Your arm should rest gently by your side. His grip on you should be firm, but not tight. This position naturally places the blind person one half step behind the guide for normal walking. This position enables you to communicate any movement to that person through minimal movement of your arm and body.

(b) Approach travel situations directly. Avoid angular approaches (other than 90 degrees) to curbs, doorways, and steps.

(c) In approaching narrow openings, such as doorways or congested areas in hallways, you, as guide, should move your elbow in a rear direction toward the center of your back. This signal indicates that the blind person should fully extend his arm and move somewhat behind you. (A verbal cue may *initially* accompany this gesture.) This change in position (fully extended arm) increases the distance between the guide and guided from one-half step to one step, and prevents the blind person from stepping on your heels.

(d) When approaching curbs and steps, you, as guide should walk up as close to the object as possible and then come to a slight pause before ascending or descending. (Use the sighted guide technique.)

(e) In guiding a person up stairs, walk one step ahead of him at a normal pace and in a rhythmic gait. Avoid stopping on the stairs. The toes of the blind person will briefly touch the vertical edge of each stair as he ascends it. He will feel the landing when reached through the repositioning of your body in relation to his.

(f) In guiding a person down stairs, walk one step ahead of him at a normal pace and in a rhythmic gait. Hesitate briefly before descending, then make a *deliberate* move down the stairs until you reach the landing.

(g) When approaching stairs equipped with a banister, you may direct the blind person to the banister. He can follow the banister (one-handed) as he moves up or down to the next floor level.

(h) A young blind child (preschool, and grades 1 and 2) may be guided by the hand until mature enough to adapt to the sighted guide technique.

(i) The guide should not give a "play-by-play account" of everything he sees while guiding his companion. Pertinent changes in terrain or events of interest, however, may be discussed. The therapist is a guide, not a "leader." Be of assistance, but promote independence to ability in your blind companion. Be discrete in your helping behavior.

(j) When showing a blind person to a chair, approach it squarely from behind. Put his hand on the back of the chair. He should check the chair for objects in the seat (you can, too), then easily seat himself.

(k) When entering a car, a blind person can usually engineer his own actions once the guide approaches the automobile at the door. Many times the statement, "Here is the car," is sufficient.

(l) Avoid becoming "mechanical" in your actions once you become efficient in sighted guide techniques. Be a companion as well as a guide. Remain as socially inconspicuous in your aid as possible. This will be appreciated by your blind companion.

(m) If a situation becomes awkward, your sense of humor is your best friend. A humorous statement on your part may relieve any tension which may arise as part of your initial experiences as a sighted guide.

IF ANY OF THE ABOVE SUGGESTIONS ANNOY YOUR BLIND COMPANION, DISREGARD THEM AND GUIDE HIM IN A MUTUALLY DESIRABLE, SAFE, MANNER.

Mannerisms in Congenitally Blind Children

Educators of the blind have used the terms mannerism and blindism interchangeably to describe noninstrumental, maladaptive patterns of behavior often exhibited by congenitally blind children. *Mannerisms* common to functionally blind children include repeated (a) rocking of the body backward and forward, (b) placing of fists or fingers into eyes, (c) shaking of fingers in front of the face, and (d) movement of the head from side to side (Morse, 1965). The term, *blindism*, may be an inappropriate descriptor, as it implies that these repetitive behaviors are exhibited only by the blind, when in fact, some sighted children manifest these actions. Knight (1972) describes *mannerisms* as noninstrumental, gross motor activities developed in infancy by all children as means of coping with tensions created by frustration, excitement, and deprivation of other stimulation. He explains that self-stimulatory behaviors are normal to infant development, but he indicates that these behaviors are abandoned by the sighted child as he begins to develop more functional behaviors. The sighted child experiences less need for noninstrumental behavior when he learns to reach outside himself to fulfill his needs. When the blind child has difficulty learning effective techniques for reducing tension, he may fulfill his needs by regressing to familiar movements as a means of relieving tension and experiencing sensation. Mannerisms are the satisfying activities to which the blind child withdraws (Caetano & Kauffman, 1975; Knight, 1972).

Some educators have attempted to reduce or eliminate the mannerisms of the blind child by substituting task-oriented, age-appropriate activities. This approach has achieved limited success, perhaps because the child is engaged in self-stimulation behavior "to such high frequency and intensity that he is not attentive to external cues" (Caetano & Kauffman, 1972, p. 102). A study by Caetano and Kauffman (1972) determined that a blind child who desires to extinguish feedback and abnormal rocking behavior may do so over time, if he is informed of the behavior each time it occurs. Approval given in response to appropriate behavior can be an effective means of assuring that the behavior reoccurs. These researchers have also suggested that a desirable activity earned in the absence of noninstrumental behavior decreases the frequency of the inappropriate behavior. Music remains a desirable means of sensory stimulation for many individuals. Therefore, music activities should be utilized as approval activities with blind children who are working to reduce these ritualistic behaviors.

Teaching Motor Skills

Movement lends itself to music, and it is an integral part of music therapy. The music therapist is effective in teaching movement to develop motor skills and to promote self-expression. Effective instruction in skills which enable movement and exploration can have a significant impact on the success experienced by the blind child in a sighted society. Success or lack thereof in movement significantly affects all other areas of human development. When working with visually disabled children, it is in teaching motor skills that the music therapist finds his greatest challenge and ultimate reward. The child without movement lives in a very small world. When he achieves effective movement, he has power at his fingertips.

DEVELOPMENT OF SOCIO-EMOTIONAL SKILLS

Emotional adjustment is not easy to define, as the factors which influence human feelings are difficult to measure. Emotional development is affected by *external events* comprised of cultural beliefs and human events, and *internal conditions*, or feelings, which are difficult to observe and occur without prediction. Emotional well-being implies (a) definition of self, (b) a sense of group belonging, (c) a sense of self in relation to play and work, and (d) a recognition of personal ability and limitation. Emotional and social adjustment are linked, in that perception of self is mirrored in the responses of others toward him. For the purpose of this discussion, emotional and social development are combined as they seem integrated beyond clear definition.

Activites common to music therapy traditionally foster enhanced self-concept and provide social interaction. Music experiences provide a structure which demands that the child organize himself through demonstration of task-oriented behavior. These activities provide for nonverbal and verbal expression of self through movement and song (Sears, 1968). Participation in group music activity provides a structure to encourage peer interaction, suppression of individual needs for the fulfillment of group needs, and opportunities to exercise communication skills. (For an in-depth discussion of the functions of music in the development of emotional and social skills, see the section on Music Therapy with Children.)

Emotional and Social Growth Patterns

The social-emotional adjustment of severely visually impaired children does not directly result from visual disability, rather it is affected by the reactions of significant others to him (Harley, 1979; Lowenfield, 1973). If a child experiences support, challenge, and success in his interactions with others, he will develop a healthy self-concept and become well-socialized. If such is not the case, low self-esteem and social maladjustment may result. Therefore, relationships with significant others must be nurtured in early childhood.

Socialization begins at birth when an infant is "bonded" to his parents. While a strong family relationship is important for the growth of any child, it is especially important for the blind child. His parents form a link to a world which is not only foreign, but unseen. The parents of a blind child serve as his eyes and provide the stimuli which will motivate his interaction with persons and things. Close physical contact, which is a key to the bonding process, is frequently denied to the visually impaired infant. The newborn's often delicate condition may require that he remain in sterile hospital isolation for observation and special care. The child's re-entry into the lives of his parents may be the beginning of a difficult adjustment to home life for all concerned.

The older visually impaired child may become frustrated when seeking meaningful relationships outside the home. His disability makes it difficult to learn socially acceptable behavior. Peers may avoid him because they misunderstand him. The child may need to prove himself if he is to be accepted by his peers. It is often these types of emotional and social experiences that the disabled child brings with him to music therapy.

Participation in music groups by sighted and visually impaired children will provide the contact necessary to initiate friendships. Further, because the musical skills of some visually disabled children are equal to or more developed than those of their sighted peers, the musically capable blind child who displays these skills will gain the respect of his sighted peers. Music activity can promote social development of visually impaired children.

Teaching Emotional and Social Awareness

When teaching skills which will enable the visually impaired child to function emotionally and socially in an effective manner, the music therapist should (a) be aware of experiential "gaps" in the child's background, (b) observe the child in as many social interactions as possible to accurately assess levels of social functioning, (c) consider the child's social strengths and reinforce these behaviors, (d) be sensitive to the frustrations that arise when the disabled child seeks to "fit in" with his peers and lacks important social information, (e) structure activities in the child's own environment which will allow the child to practice and ask questions about socially appropriate behavior, (f) teach socially appropriate ways of expressing emotion, (g) encourage the development of personal habits which will lead to social acceptance outside the blind community, (h) encourage independent functioning to ability, and (i) structure the immediate environment so that the child learns to accept and compensate for his handicapping condition.

The severely visually impaired child learns at some point in his development that he is different from other children. He learns through experience that healthy social interaction is a desirable activity and he wants to "fit in." However, the child's social experiences may have been difficult and unrewarding in many instances. Although wanting to be a part of the social community, he is often unwilling to risk the interaction, especially with sighted peers. In teaching skills which will facilitate health, emotional, and social development, the music therapist serves to structure and support positive experiences.

REFERENCE NOTES

1. The program contributed by Doreen Veazie-Desmangles, RMT, Oak Hill School, Connecticut Institute for the Blind.

2. Case study contributed by Doreen Veazie-Desmangles, RMT, Oak Hill School, Connecticut Institute for the Blind.

3. Many of the goals in this and the following sections were developed by a team of educators, including the author, at the Tennessee School for the Blind in Danelson, Tennessee. In 1976, a comprehensive assessment tool was developed at the school for use in assessing progress and planning curricula for children with a wide range of abilities. The guide was a pilot project sponsored by the Elementary and Secondary Act 89-313-10 of the Office of Special Education which sponsored an extensive revision of the tool in 1979, following a three-year test period. These goals were adapted for use in this monograph.

REFERENCES

Baratta-Lorton, M. *Activity-centered learning in the home: Workjobs for parents.* Menlo Park, CA: Addison-Wesley, 1975.

Birkenshaw, L. *Music for fun, music for learning* (2nd ed.). Toronto: Holt, Rinehart, and Winston, 1977.

Bitcon, C. *Alike and different: The clinical and educational use of Orff-Schulwerk.* Santa Ana, CA: Rosha Press, 1976.

Braley, W., Konicki, G. & Leedy, C. (Eds.) *Daily sensorimotor training activities: A handbook for teachers and parents of preschool children.* New York: Educational Activities, 1968.

Caetano, A. & Kauffman, J. Reduction of rocking mannerisms in two blind children. *Education of the Visually Handicapped,* 1975, 7, 101-105.

Cartwright, G. & Cartwright, C. *CARE: Early identification of handicapped children.* University Park, PA: Pennsylvania State University, 1972, and revised for *A systems personnel development* (ASPD). Iowa City: University of Iowa, 1980.

Coker, G. & Dhindsa, H. (Eds.) *Comprehensive curriculum guide for multihandicapped children* (Developed as a Pilot Project sponsored by the Elementary and Secondary Act No. 89-313-10 of the federal government). Donelson, TN: Tennessee School for the Blind, 1979.

Duerksen, G. *General uses of music in working with handicapped children.* Unpublished manuscript, 1978.

Eagle, C. *Music therapy for handicapped children and youth: An annotated and indexed bibliography.* Lawrence, KS: National Association for Music Therapy, 1982.

Federal register, August 23, 1977.

Gaston, E. Man and music. In E. Gaston (Ed.), *Music in therapy.* New York: Macmillan, 1968.

Graham, R. Music education of emotionally disturbed children. In R. Graham (Compiler), *Music for the exceptional child.* Reston, VA: Music Educators National Conference, 1975.

Harley, R. *Moderate and severe visual disabilities.* Unpublished monograph, Peabody College for Teachers, 1979.

Harley, R. & Lawrence, G. *Visual impairment in the schools.* Springfield, IL: Charles C Thomas, 1977.

Jacobson, E. *You must relax.* New York: McGraw-Hill, 1970.

Klebanoff, H. *Home stimulation for the young developmentally disabled child* (Developed as a grant project of PL 91-517, Massachusetts State Plan for Services and Facilities for the Developmentally Disabled). Lexington, MA: 1973.

Knight, J. Mannerisms in the congenitally blind child. *New Outlook for the Blind,* 1972, 66(9), 297-302.

Kratz, L. *Movement without sight: Physical activity and dance for the visually handicapped.* Palo Alto, CA: Peek Publications, 1977.

Lathom, W. *Role of music therapy in the education of handicapped children and youth.* Lawrence, KS: National Association for Music Therapy, 1980.

Lowenfeld, B. (Ed.) *The visually handicapped child in school.* New York: John Day, 1973.

Meyen, E. *Exceptional children and youth: An introduction.* Denver: Love Publishing, 1978.

Michel, D. *Music therapy: An introduction to therapy and special education through music.* Springfield, IL: Charles C Thomas, 1976.

Morse, J. Mannerisms, not blindness: Causation and treatment. *The Education of the Blind,* 1965, 12-16.

Nolan, C. The visually impaired. In E. Meyen (Ed.), *Exceptional children and youth: An introduction.* Denver: Love Publishing, 1978.

Purvis, J. & Samet, S. *Developmental music therapy.* Lawrence, KS: National Association for Music Therapy, 1974.

Purvis, J. & Samet, S. (Eds.) *Music in developmental therapy: A curriculum guide.* Baltimore: University Park Press, 1976.

Ross, R. *Speech communication: Fundamentals and practice.* Englewood Cliffs, NJ: Prentice-Hall, 1980.

Sears, W. Processes in music therapy. In E. Gaston (Ed.), *Music in therapy.* New York: MacMillan, 1968.

Selye, H. *The stress of life.* New York: McGraw-Hill, 1956.

Vaughan, D. *General ophthalmology.* Los Altos, CA: Lange Medical Publications, 1968.

Vise, N. *Orientation and mobility in the primary grades taught through the media of rhythms, dance exercises and body movement exercises.* A Specialists Paper presented to the Department of Special Education, George Peabody College of Teachers, Nashville, Tennessee, 1972.

Wood, M. (Ed.) *Developmental therapy.* Baltimore: University Park Press, 1975.

Wood, M. (Ed.) *The Rutland Center model for treating emotionally disturbed children.* Athens, GA: Technical Assistance Office, Rutland Center, 1972.

BIBLIOGRAPHY

General

Arena, J. (Ed.) *Teaching through sensory-motor experiences.* San Rafael, CA: Academic Therapy Publications, 1969.

Carolan, R. Sensory stimulation and the blind infant. *New Outlook for the Blind,* 1973, *67*(3), 119-126.

Carolan, R. Sensory stimulation in the nursing home. *New Outlook for the Blind,* 1973, *67*(3), 126-130.

Cratty, B. *Perceptual and motor development in infants and children.* London: Collier-Macmillan, 1970.

Cratty, B. & Hutton, R. *Experiments in movement behavior and motor learning.* Philadelphia: Lea and Febiger, 1969.

Cratty, B. & Sams, T. *The body image of blind children.* New York: American Foundation for the Blind, 1968.

Cutsforth, T. *The blind school and society.* New York: American Foundation for the Blind, 1951.

Frostig, M. Visual perception, integrative functions and academic learning. *Journal of Learning Disabilities,* 1972, *5*(1), 1-15.

Hart, V. *Beginning with the handicapped.* Springfield, IL: Charles C Thomas, 1974.

Kephart, J., Kephart, C. & Schwartz, G. A journey into the world of the blind child. *Exceptional Children,* 1974, *40*(6), 421-427.

Lydon, W. & McGraw, M. *Concept development for visually handicapped children: A resource guide for teachers and other professionals working in educational settings.* New York: American Foundation for the Blind, 1973.

Piaget, J. *The child and reality: Problems of genetic psychology.* New York: Grossman Publishers, 1973.

Thomas, C. & Thomas, J. *Meeting the needs of the handicapped: A resource for teachers and librarians.* Phoenix, AZ: Oryx Press, 1980.

Warren, D. *Blindness and early childhood development.* New York: American Foundation for the Blind, 1977.

Music

Arje, F. & Berryman, D. New help for the severely retarded and emotionally disturbed child. *Journal of Rehabilitation,* 1966, *32*(1), 14-67.

Blos, J. Rhymes, song, records and stories: Language learning experiences for preschool blind children. *New Outlook for the Blind,* 1974, *68*(7), 300-307.

Coates, E. Music for the blind and physically handicapped from the Library of Congress. *The American Music Teacher,* 1976, *25*(4), 21-24.

Crockford, C. Making the most of rhythm and song: An invitation to the withdrawn child. *Journal of the Canadian Association for Music Therapy,* 1977, *5*(2), 7-8.

Dryer, J. & Dix, J. Reaching the blind child through music therapy. *Journal of Emotional Education,* 1968, *8*(4), 202-211.

Goodenough, F. & Goodenough, D. The importance of music in the life of a visually handicapped child. *Education for the Visually Handicapped,* 1970, *2*(1), 28-32.

Herlein, D. Music reading of the sightless—Braille notation. *Music Educators Journal,* 1975, *62*(1), 42-45.

Kondorossy, E. Let their music speak for the handicapped. *Music Educators Journal,* 1966, *52*(4), 115-119.

Lewis, M. A handbell choir for blind students. *New Outlook for the Blind,* 1974, *68*(7), 297-299.

Matteson, A. Finding the self in space: More than one handicap doesn't make less than one child. *Music Educators Journal,* 1972, *58*(8), 63-65.

Mooney, K. Blind children need training, not sympathy. *Music Educators Journal,* 1972, *58*(8), 56-59.

Morgan, W. Hearing is believing: Auditorium and music building. Kentucky School for the Blind, Louisville. *Progressive Architecture,* 1978, *59*(4), 86-89.

Nebe, H. Music therapy: Its function in supporting the rehabilitation of the handicapped. *Journal of Music Therapy,* 1971, *8*(2), 3-11.

Nocera, S. *Reaching the special learner through music.* Morristown, NJ: Silver Burdett, 1979.

Robbins, J. & Robbins, F. *Educational rhythmics.* New York: Association Press, 1964.

Shepherd, L. & Simons, G. Music training for the visually handicapped. *Music Educators Journal,* 1970, *56*(6), 80-81.

Smeets, P. The effects of various sounds and noise levels on stereotyped rocking of blind retardates. *Training School Bulletin,* 1972, *68*, 221-226.

Stoesz, G. & Bowers, R. Early piano instruction for partially seeing children. *Sight Saving Review,* 1965, *31*(1), 24-26.

Tillinghast, J. Developmental arts for exceptional children: Program report. (Oklahoma Children's Memorial Hospital, Child Study Center, Oklahoma City). *Journal of Clinical Child Psychology,* 1977, *6*(3), 96-97.

Zinar, R. Music in the mainstream. *Teacher,* 1978, *95*(7), 54-56.

Music Therapy

Alley, J. Education for the severely handicapped: The role of music therapy. *Journal of Music Therapy,* 1977, *14*(2), 50-59.

Alley, J. Music in the IEP: Therapy/education. *Journal of Music Therapy,* 1979, *16*(3), 111-127.

Appell, M. Arts for the handicapped: A researchable item. *Journal of Music Therapy,* 1980, *17*(2), 75-83.

Cassity, M. The influence of a socially valued skill on peer acceptance in a music therapy group. *Journal of Music Therapy,* 1981, *18*(3), 148-154.

Cassity, M. Nontraditional guitar techniques for the educable and trainable mentally retarded residents in music therapy activities. *Journal of Music Therapy,* 1977, *14*(1), 39-42.

Cassity, M. Social development of TMRs involved in performing and nonperforming groups. *Journal of Music Therapy,* 1978, *15*(2), 100-105.

Cohen, G., Averbach, J. & Katz, E. Music therapy assessment of the developmentally disabled client. *Journal of Music Therapy,* 1978, *15*(2), 88-99.

Geringer, J. An assessment of children's musical instrument preferences. *Journal of Music Therapy,* 1977, *14*(4), 172-179.

Greenwald, M. The effectiveness of distorted music versus interrupted music to decrease self-stimulatory behaviors in profoundly retarded adolescents. *Journal of Music Therapy,* 1978, *15*(2), 58-66.

Greer, R. Contributions of the psychology of music to music education and music therapy. *Journal of Music Therapy,* 1974, *11*(4), 208-219.

Greer, R. Music instruction as behavior modification. *Journal of Music Therapy,* 1976, *13*(3), 130-141.

Hanser, S. Group-contingent music listening with emotionally disturbed boys. *Journal of Music Therapy,* 1974, *11*(4), 220-225.

Holloway, M. A comparison of passive and active music reinforcement to increase pre-academic and motor skills in severely retarded children and adolescents. *Journal of Music Therapy,* 1980, *17*(2), 58-69.

Humphrey, T. The effect of music ear training upon the auditory discrimination abilities of trainable mentally retarded adolescents. *Journal of Music Therapy,* 1980, *17*(2), 70-74.

Jellison, J. Accuracy of temporal order recall for verbal and song digit-spans presented to right and left ears. *Journal of Music Therapy,* 1976, *13*(3), 114-129.

Jellison, J. The music therapist in the educational setting: Developing and implementing curriculum for the handicapped. *Journal of Music Therapy,* 1979, *16*(3), 128-137.

Kramer, S. The effects of music as a cue in maintaining handwashing in preschool children. *Journal of Music Therapy,* 1978, *15*(3), 136-144.

Larson, A. Auditory and visual rhythmic pattern recognition by emotionally disturbed and normal adolescents. *Journal of Music Therapy,* 1981, *18*(3), 128-136.

Lienhard, M. Factors relevant to the rhythmic perception of a group of mentally retarded children. *Journal of Music Therapy,* 1976, *13*(2), 58-65.

Madsen, C., Moore, R., Wagner, M. & Yarbrough, C. A comparison of music as reinforcement for correct mathematical responses versus music as reinforcement for attentiveness. *Journal of Music Therapy,* 1975, *12*(2), 84-95.

Madsen, C. & Wolfe, D. The effect of interrupted music and incompatible responses on bodily movement and music attentiveness. *Journal of Music Therapy,* 1979, *16*(2), 17-30.

Myers, E. The effect of music on retention in a paired-associate task with EMR children. *Journal of Music Therapy,* 1979, *16*(4), 190-198.

Rider, S. The assessment of cognitive functioning level through musical perception. *Journal of Music Therapy,* 1981, *18*(3), 110-119.

Rohner, S. & Miller, R. Degrees of familiar and affective music and their effects on state anxiety. *Journal of Music Therapy,* 1980, *17*(1), 2-15.

Rubin, B. Handbells in therapy. *Journal of Music Therapy,* 1976, *13*(1), 49-53.

Saperston, B., Chan, R., Morphew, C. & Carsrud, K. Music listening versus juice as a reinforcement for learning in profoundly mentally retarded individuals. *Journal of Music Therapy,* 1980, *17*(4), 174-183.

Staum, M. An analysis of movement in therapy. *Journal of Music Therapy,* 1981, *18*(1), 7-24.

Wilson, C. & Aiken, L. The effects of intensity levels upon physiological and subjective affective response to rock music. *Journal of Music Therapy,* 1977, *14*(2), 60-76.

Wolfe, D. The effect of automated interrupted music on head posturing of cerebral palsied individuals. *Journal of Music Therapy,* 1980, *17*(4), 184-206.

SELECTED READINGS AND RESOURCES

American Printing House catalogs and resources. American Printing House for the Blind.

Barbara, D., et al. *Teaching aids for blind and visually limited children.* American Foundation for the Blind.

Barraga, N., et al. *Aids for teaching basic concepts of sensory development.* American Printing House for the Blind, No. 700225.

Bortner, S., et al. *Sensory stimulation kit.* American Printing House for the Blind.

Bortner, S., et al. *Sensory stimulation kit: A teacher's guidebook* (to accompany above kit). American Printing House for the Blind, No. 8-1185.

Can make and do books: Look, listen, touch, taste, smell, etc. Waco, TX: Wilt, Joy, and Terre Watson Creative Resources.

Gordon, B., et al. *Instruction guide for teachers of the blind.* Seattle Public Schools: Administrative and Service Center, 815 Fourth Avenue North, Seattle, WA 98109.

Harlein, D. Music reading for the sightless: Braille notation. *Music Educators Journal,* 1975, *62*(1), 42-45.

Home stimulation for the young developmentally disabled child. Lexington, MA: Commonwealth Mental Health Foundation.

Instruction in music for visually handicapped children (Vol. 1). 301 Ashe Avenue, Raleigh, NC 27605.

May, M. *Nonverbal communication and the congenitally blind: A subject bibliography of print and non-print materials for the development of training programs.* American Foundation for the Blind, 1977.

Palmer, H. *Getting to know myself* (LP album no. 543). Freeport, NY: Activity Records; Educational Activities, 1972.

Portage guide to early education (with developmental checklist). Portage, WI: Cooperative Educational Service Agency, Number 12.

Quigley, H., et al. *Instruction guide for teachers of the partially seeing.* Seattle Public Schools: Administrative and Service Center, 815 Fourth Avenue North, Seattle, WA 98109.

Recorded aid for braille music. Paper no. 3. The prospectus series. East Lansing, MI: Michigan State University, Regional Instructional Materials Center for Handicapped Children and Youth.

Talking books (children and adults). Washington: Library of Congress, Division for the Blind and Physically Handicapped.

Volunteers who produce books: Braille, large type, tape. Washington: U.S. Government Printing Office, 1973.

SUPPORT ORGANIZATIONS

American Foundation for the Blind, Inc.
15 West Sixteenth Street
New York, New York 10011

Provides a wide variety of services for visually handicapped persons including a special reference library on blindness. Conducts and stimulates research to determine the most effective methods of serving visually handicapped persons.

American Printing House for the Blind, Inc.
1839 Frankfort Avenue
Louisville, Kentucky 40206

National organization for the production of literature and the manufacture of educational materials for visually handicapped students. Receives an appropriation from Congress to provide textbooks and educational aids for all registered students attending schools and/or other special education institutions of less than college grade. Publishes braille books, music, and magazines; large type textbooks; talking books and magazines; cassette tapes; and educational tape recordings. Manufactures special educational aids for blind and visually handicapped persons. Maintains an educational research and development program concerned with not only educational procedures and methods, but also the development of educational aids. Provides audio equipment to students for educational purposes.

Association for Education of the Visually Handicapped
919 Walnut Street
Philadelphia, Pennsylvania 19107

Professional organization open to persons professionally involved in the education of visually handicapped persons. Assists in efforts to improve material and methods of teaching visually handicapped persons.

Division for the Visually Handicapped
Council for Exceptional Children
1920 Association Drive
Reston, Virginia 22091

Professional organization of teachers and others concerned with children who require special services. Publishes periodicals, books, and other materials on teaching the exceptional child.

APPENDIX A

OAK HILL SCHOOL
conducted by
The Connecticut Institute for the Blind

MUSIC THERAPY: INITIAL EVALUATION FORM*

DATE **9-10-80**

NAME **Bert**   DATE OF BIRTH **12-21-60**   AGE **19**

HANDICAP(s) **Blindness, mental retardation, double scoliosis**

MOBILITY **independent** SIGHT **light perception** (questionable) HEARING **yes** SPEECH **sign language** (vocalizations)

EMOTIONAL RESPONSE **even-tempered** SELF STIMULATING BEHAVIORS **body rocks**

COMMENTS **walks with shuffled gait, becomes easily frustrated**

RHYTHMIC RESPONSE

Clap Hands _____ independently
    ✓ with help
    _____ in rhythm
    _____ with therapist
    _____ N/A

Feet _____ kept time with music
    ✓ independently
    _____ with help
    _____ seated
    _____ standing
    _____ in motion
    _____ N/A

Gross
Motor _____ sway
    ✓ rock
    ✓ walk
    _____ run
    _____ jump
    _____ skip

INSTRUMENT PREFERENCE
(indicated by physical or verbal response)

_____ sticks   _____ melodica
_____ tone block   _____ piano
_____ temple blocks   _____ electric piano
_____ maracas   _____ w/headset
_____ claves   ✓ glockenspiel
_____ sand blocks   _____ resonator bells
_____ bells   _____ bass xylophone
✓ triangle   _____ alto xylophone
_____ finger cymbals   _____ soprano xylophone
_____ large cymbals   _____ pentatonic xylophone
_____ gong
_____ tom-tom
_____ bongo
✓ tambourine
_____ tympani
_____ Autoharp
_____ double bass
_____ guitar
_____ recorder

RECORDED MUSIC
Instrumental **Body Rocks**
Vocal _____

"LIVE" MUSIC
Instrumental **will beat rhythmically**
Vocal **smiles when therapist sings**

COMMENTS **Best learning mode: auditory / motor**

---

* Devised by Sr. Lucille J. Cormier, C.N.D., R.M.T. of Misericordia College
  for Conn. Institute for the Blind

APPENDIX B

OAK HILL SCHOOL
conducted by
The Connecticut Institute for the Blind
MUSIC THERAPY: **BASELINE CHECKLIST***

NAME __Bert__   DATE __✓ 9-23-80__ / __+ 9-14-81__

GROSS MOTOR

- _____ no independent movement _____
- ✓ walk _____ +
- _____ run _____
- ✓ rock _____ +
- _____ sway _____ +
- _____ jump _____
- _____ skip _____
- ✓ hand clapping _____ +
- _____ imitation _____
- _____ balance _____ +

FINE MOTOR

- _____ no independent response _____
- _____ visual tracking _____
- _____ eye/hand coordination _____
- _____ visual/auditory _____
- _____ visual/motor _____
- ✓ hand grasp _____ +
- _____ pincer grasp _____ +

AUDITORY SKILLS

- ✓ physical reaction _____
- _____ deliberate response _____ +
- _____ reaches toward source _____ +
- _____ imitates (vocal) _____ +
- _____ imitates rhythm _____ +
- _____ sequential memory _____ +
- _____ position in space _____
- _____ remembers story content _____

SOCIALIZATION

- _____ interacts w/therapist _____ +
- _____ appropriate (meaningful) conversation _____
- _____ game w/peers _____
- _____ game w/therapist _____ +
- _____ tolerates touch _____ +
- _____ tolerates texture _____ +
- _____ eye contact _____

COMMUNICATION

- _____ no response _____
- _____ babbles _____
- _____ eye contact _____
- _____ reach for object _____ +
- _____ reach for therapist _____ +
- _____ respond to sign w/action _____
- _____ respond to sign w/sign _____
- _____ match object to picture _____
- _____ match picture to picture _____
- _____ match picture to object _____
- _____ word approximation _____ +

- ✓ follows one-part command _____ +
- _____ follows two-part command _____ +
- _____ follows three-part command _____
- _____ uses language board _____
- _____ uses natural gesture _____ +
- _____ understands simple commands _____ +
- _____ completes phrase/sentence _____ +
- _____ asks for needs _____
- ✓ receptive skills better than expressive

*Devised by Sr. Lucille J. Cormier, C.N.D., R.M.T., of Misericorida College
for the Conn. Institute for the Blind

BODY PARTS

- ✔ head ___ +
- ✔ hair ___ +
- ✔ ears ___ +
- ___ eyes ___ +
- ✔ nose ___ +
- ✔ mouth ___ +
- ___ face ___ +
- ✔ chin ___ +
- ___ neck ___ +
- ✔ stomach ___ +
- ___ chest ___ +
- ___ back ___ +
- ___ side ___
- ___ legs ___ +
- ___ knees ___ +
- ___ ankles ___
- ✔ feet ___ +
- ___ toes ___ +
- ✔ arms ___ +
- ___ elbows ___ +
- ___ wrist ___
- ___ hands ___ +
- ___ fingers ___
- ___ shoulders ___

CONCEPTS

- ✔ up ___ +
- ✔ down ___ +
- ___ loud ___ +
- ___ soft ___ +
- ✔ fast ___ +
- ✔ slow ___ +
- ___ on ___
- ___ under ___
- ___ over ___
- ___ same ___
- ___ different ___
- ___ next to ___
- ___ beside ___
- ___ in front of ___
- ___ in back of ___ +
- ___ behind ___
- ___ big ___ +
- ___ small ___ +
- ___ push ___
- ___ turn ___
- ___ tap ___
- ✔ shake ___ +
- ✔ clap ___ +

BEHAVIOR

- ✔ self-stimulation ___
- ___ tolerance for frustration ___ +
- ___ adaptation to change ___ +
- ___ temper tantrums ___
- ___ self-abusive behavior ___
- ___ perseveration in speech ___
- ___ perseveration in action ___
- ___ hyperactive ___
- ___ aggressive toward peers
- ___ aggressive toward therapist ___

ATTENTION SPAN

- ___ eye contact ___
- ___ attends to therapist's face ___
- ___ easily distracted ___
- ___ on task ___ +

COMMENTS ✔ Responds to music with hand-clapping, smiles and vocalizations

+ Will trail room with verbal cue; does well with gesture songs; signs for many instruments: drum, tambourine, triangle, music, dance.

MONOGRAPH 3

MUSIC THERAPY FOR
DEAF-BLIND CHILDREN

Sr. Lucille J. Cormier

IDENTIFYING THE DISABILITY

The education of deaf-blind children gained recognition and promise in the 19th century. Although occasional reports of the incidence of the dual impairment may be found in literature of the 17th and 18th centuries, it was not until the plight of Julia Brace (1807-1884), Laura Bridgman (1829-1876), and Helen Keller of more recent history became known, that the possibility of education for the multihandicapped child was given serious consideration.

During the 1930s and 1940s, some gains were made in the education of a few deaf-blind children. However, it was not until 1953 that The National Study Committee on the Education of Deaf-Blind Children was established (Waterhouse, 1977). The founding of this organization was the first sign of long-range planning of educational services for multihandicapped children.

The rubella epidemic of the 1960s caused a vast increase in the number of deaf-blind children throughout the world. As a result of the epidemic in this country, "an estimated 30,000 children were born with one or more handicaps including visual impairment, hearing impairment, mental retardation, and a variety of other physical disabilities" (Dantona, 1976, p. 55). The rubella virus is one of several causes of deaf-blindness. Other causes include congenital and hereditary factors, disease, and adventitious trauma.

The increase in the deaf-blind population in so few years is quite significant in terms of how these children are to be educated. Congress responded to the severity of the problem by approving a plan to develop regional deaf-blind centers. By 1970, ten regional centers had been established, serving all of the United States. By 1976, funding had increased to sixteen million dollars, providing help to parents and teachers of deaf-blind children. Through these centers, deaf-blind children were identified and provided with diagnostic, evaluation, and placement services. These centers are not educational facilities, but serve in an administrative and resource capacity (Dantona, 1974).

How are professionals to determine who should be identified as deaf-blind?

The deaf-blind child is defined as a child who has auditory and visual handicaps, the combination of which causes such severe communication problems that they cannot properly be accommodated in special education programs solely for the hearing handicapped or for the visually handicapped (Dantona, 1976, p. 56).

There are some implications to be derived from this definition. A child may be diagnosed as legally deaf-blind or clinically deaf-blind. Legal blindness consists of visual acuity of 20/200 or less in the better eye with correction. Legal blindness also includes persons whose visual acuity is stated as better than 20/200, but having a limited central field of vision (Holm, 1979).

There is no legal definition for hearing impairment; it is normally categorized according to severity, from mild to profound. Profoundly hearing-impaired persons are considered to be deaf.

Formerly, deafness was diagnosed as mild, moderate, severe, or profound. Except for the profoundly deaf, recent audiological journals consider all other categories as hearing-impaired. However, for the sake of simplicity, those with both hearing *and* vision impairments are referred to as deaf-blind.

Clinically, or functionally, persons are diagnosed deaf-blind when their auditory mechanisms appear to be intact, but due to brain damage, are unable to process incoming visual or auditory stimuli, in effect, causing deaf-blindness.

The observer of a deaf-blind child witnesses the fact that, besides the already mentioned handicaps, this child is also without language. It is understandable, then, why it becomes imperative that all means available be used through which a child can become self-expressive and socialized, and can share in the human aspects of order and meaning.

Behaviorally, the deaf-blind child exhibits behaviors which are similar to those of a child who might be diagnosed as autistic. For example, there is little or no recognition of human relationships in the more seriously impaired deaf-blind child. Furthermore, there is little interest in objects, except when these objects serve to enhance the child's most prominent behavioral characteristic (i.e., light gazing). The deaf-blind child has a fanatic obsession with light. Constant restlessness, distractibility, and impulsiveness also contribute to the child's difficulty in learning. Finger flicking, arm flapping, and rocking are to be included in the list of behavioral characteristics.

Children whose visual and hearing deficits are caused by postnatal illness or trauma are less deficit in intellectual functioning than those whose handicapping condition is caused by prenatal insult. Prenatal causes such as rubella virus usually contribute to serious neurological problems, mental retardation, and behavioral abnormalities. The high percentage of very low functioning deaf-blind children is an indicator that professionals and parents responsible for their education must be as creative and daring as their minds allow them to be in the effort to reach as many children as possible, in as effective a manner as possible.

When comparing a deaf-blind child to a normal child, one is immediately overwhelmed by the multihandicapped child's passivity and lack of curiosity about the environment. The deaf-blind child frequently resists all forms of interaction and touch from another. Self-abusive behavior is common. This is more easily understood when one considers that the child is deprived of the normal functioning of both distance senses: hearing and vision. These are essential channels for the acquisition of environmental information and all that it implies—curiosity, experimentation, and the appropriate responses of joy, anger, fear, trust, playfulness, etc.

Essentially, the deaf-blind child learns through movement and the near sense of touch, with some input attributed to taste and smell. The normal child first learns through visual and auditory awareness, as these provide new and exciting sounds, shapes, colors, and objects to be explored. The normal child's mobility often begins because of an object seen or heard which motivates the child to go after it. The deaf-blind child, on the other hand, must wait until someone presents an object and helps in the exploration of it, because the child does not have sufficient vision and hearing to be stimulated independently. Even movement for the deaf-blind child usually is initiated by another.

While some of the deaf-blind children's lack of curiosity is due to limited visual and auditory stimulation, these children most often also have neurological impairments limiting ability to relate cause and effect. There must be an intermediary to help these children experience the combination of environmental cause and effect and the impact it has on their person. This intermediary may be in the form of another person or a skill.

Motor and social development in deaf-blind children are perhaps the slowest and most difficult to attain. The reality of the child's handicaps begins an emotional strain within the family unit. The multiplicity of professional personnel encountered in the course of the educational process also contributes to the child's confusion and insecurity when exposed to inconsistent methods of interaction. Even if the problem encountered within the family and educational settings were eliminated, deaf-blind children could not establish relationships easily because of the severity of handicapping conditions.

It is not possible, nor fair, to attempt chronological developmental comparisons between normal children and deaf-blind children. There are too many variables to consider. However, there are some general similarities. Developmental lags and splinter skills are prevalent in all children. A splinter skill is a performance learned in a specific manner to satisfy a specific need or demand. It is performed with a high degree of skill but with a minimum of flexibility. It is learned out of developmental sequence and usually cannot be generalized.

Not all children respond to stimuli in the same way, if at all. The needs, abilities, and personality of the individual child must always be taken into consideration when planning and implementing an educational program. Multihandicapped children learn more slowly and sporadically than the normal child, but like normal children, learn best when individual strengths are recognized and used to advantage. As in the development of all children, the critical ingredient for success in the development of multihandicapped children lies in the energetic creativity of the professional, coupled with sensitivity, perception, humor, hope, and genuine caring for fellow human beings.

ASSESSMENT OF THE CHILD[1]

The assessment process is one of the first and most important steps in the programming of the deaf-blind child. Total assessment, of course, is more than just testing: It is a process that attempts to discover all there is to know about the student's level of functioning and how that student learns best. Tests may be given for placement purposes, to satisfy legal requirements, and to compare one child's performance with others having similar problems. But the main purpose of assessing is to enable the teacher/therapist to develop the most appropriate program to meet the child's needs.

Two basic types of assessments need to be delineated for the sake of clarity. The first type is the performance-based assessment which is a test comprised of standard items requiring the child to carry out specific tasks or exhibit certain behaviors upon presentation of certain stimuli; these items are often timed. The second type of assessment is observation of spontaneous behaviors which is best carried out in structured and unstructured settings, observing the child alone or in a group.

Research indicates that observation measures correlate significantly with developmental scale measures for the deaf-blind, but the information obtained is not completely redundant. Both should be used (Diebold, 1978). Developmental scales tell the teacher where the child is and what the next logical step should be. Observations may substantiate or bring test results into question, but their primary purpose is to inform the teacher/therapist about how the child learns best—behaviors conducive to or interfering with learning.

As part of an interdisciplinary team, the music therapist has certain responsibilities in the assessment process. First, it is the responsibility of the therapist to be familiar with the tests commonly used with deaf-blind students. The music therapist should be informed of the results of any tests completed on the student, as well as of any assessments from other areas, such as physical therapy, occupational therapy, speech therapy, and from psychological reports. In addition, the music therapist should conduct observations of music activities in the music therapy setting. The information gained from this process should be sufficient to determine a meaningful music therapy program which will help the student toward the attainment of the long-term goals determined by the interdisciplinary team.

There are many variables to consider when assessing performance. They include:

- What is the child's primary handicapping condition?
- What impairment most affects the child's performance?
- What is the child's primary mode of learning?
- What is the child's primary means of approaching tasks and materials?
- How quickly does the child learn a task?
- What materials does the child most enjoy?
- What materials does the child least enjoy?
- What reinforcers are most effective?
- What is the child's level of comprehension?
- What are the child's strengths?
- What are the child's weaknesses?
- What is the child's developmental level?

The physical, sensory, psychological, and/or neurological disabilities associated with deaf-blind children may not only limit performances in a given test area, but may account for marked discrepancies between developmental areas. They could also account for the very different performances from one observation to the next. These reversals may be due, in part, to environmental fluctuations (such as weather, classroom, teacher) as well as physiological changes (such as EEG, chemical levels, heart rate). Medications may also play a part in performance quality.

There are complex interrelationships in the development of our senses. If any part of this complex system is not functioning properly, the result may be complete disorder. The deaf-blind person does not anticipate, and thus is not prepared to respond. Experiences are fragmented, single events and, therefore, are not integrated or related one to the other. Routines are safer and simple; repetitive tasks are preferred. If teachers or therapists try to interrupt or interfere with this routine, anger or resentment on the part of the student may result.

There are some cautions necessary in the assessment of deaf-blind children in the communication, academic, motor, and social areas. The deaf-blind child may have problems in simple imitation which is the forerunner of speech. There is a disruption of rhythm or a lack of rhythm which has a negative effect on short-term memory and thus on speech. Deafness alone does not seriously affect the sensory-motor areas except in vocal imitation, but there is a lack of awareness of the symbolic values of language which, in the normal child, emerges around the age of two.

Acquisition of academic skills depends largely on input from our senses. The blind child will be delayed in the concept of object permanence from the first month on due to the visual inability to track. The delay of concept development increases as time goes on. There is less delay in this area with children who are deaf. Blindness seems to extend the time of oral exploration for purposes of learning. Partially sighted children are likely to exhibit hand-waving behavior.

The concept of time is distorted for the deaf-blind child. In relation to this, one can expect a delay in the development of the concept of causality, such as, "if I cry, mother will come."

Touching and smelling are the gateways to learning for the deaf-blind child, but only if these senses are used for discovery. If they are only used for sensation or self-stimulation, they may inhibit learning. Smell appears to be related to emotion, and so may elicit a great deal of excitement. If the distance senses of sight and hearing are impaired, then the child must rely on the near senses of touch, taste, and smell, as well as proprioception and balance, or equilibrium.

One of the first things noticed about the deaf-blind child is limited motor activity. Motor functions are often poorly developed and much time may be wasted on stereotypic or repetitive movements. If the child is so preoccupied with his own body, then all things are perceived as extensions of self rather than as distinct objects which have their own qualities. Because of this "in-sistent" behavior, little spatial experience will be gained. Frequently, deaf-blind children also are quite motorically clumsy.

One of the very first developmental steps is to raise the head while prone. The deaf-blind child may be seriously delayed in this initial stage of development. Usually the head follows the eyes, or in the case of the visually impaired, the ears. The child hears or sees something and raises the head in order to orient toward the object. If nothing is seen or heard, then there is little motivation to accomplish this most important step.

Another very important milestone is that of reaching toward a sound, a behavior which normally occurs around the twelfth month. Until this is attained, the child will not move in space or reach out beyond himself. This may be expected to be delayed in the deaf-blind child.

As mentioned earlier, social and motor development are perhaps the most difficult for the deaf-blind child to acquire. The blind child's smiling response will be more delayed than the sighted child, since smiling to a familiar face (usually mother) is an earlier developmental step than smiling to a voice. Social development suffers overall because the two experiences of "mother" and "pleasure" cannot be related to each other. As noted, experiences are fragmented rather than integrated. Frustration experienced because of this fragmentation contributes to emotional and/or psychological difficulties commonly observed in children with the dual impairment in vision and hearing.

Guided observation in the music therapy assessment session may accomplish several purposes. The assessment should help determine preferred music and motivating music activities, and identify other possible reinforcers. It should also cue the therapist regarding student behaviors conducive to learning as well as behaviors which might interfere with learning. It will assist the therapist in determining the child's readiness for a particular activity. It will identify areas of strength that need reinforcement and generalization as well as areas of weakness that need special attention and remediation. It may also be used to structure the type of interaction between the therapist and child, which is most likely to bring about progress in the identified areas.

The following format for assessment is based on suggested procedures used in assessing cognitive behaviors developed by Uzgiris and Hung (Wabash Center for the Mentally Retarded, 1977). In the structured part of the observation, the student should be positioned so that the stimuli can be seen and heard, making a variety of responses possible. This will depend on the individual child and the particular sensory and/or motor impairments. The "games" should be started with materials that are within the child's level of functioning. If they are too low, boredom will result; if they are too high, the child may become frustrated. All of the "toys" should be close at hand. Items suggested for use in testing include: bells of various sizes and timbres, maracas or rattles, drums of various sizes and timbres, mallets, wind-up musical toys, simple wind instruments (tooters), and simple keyboard instruments. Present the instruments one at a time over a period of days, allowing plenty of time for the child to respond. This will depend on the child's attention span and interest level. If the child does not reach for or grasp the object, place it in his hand. Permit the child to play with or explore the object for up to three minutes, or until interest is lost and actions are repeated. Observe the child according to the following suggestions, and note responses:

- holds the object for more than 30 seconds.
- brings the object to mouth.
- brings the object before the eyes, or holds it and looks at it.
- hits the object with hand.
- hits the object on a surface.
- shakes or waves the object.
- hits two objects together.
- pats the object.
- examines the object.
- slides the object on a surface.
- crumples the object.
- stretches the object out.
- attempts to tear the object.
- drops the object systematically.
- throws the object.
- puts another object into it.
- demonstrates drinking from a cup.
- listens to the sound of the musical toy.
- shows the object to another person.
- points to another object in association.
- names the object.

If the child shows the same or similar response to three or more of these items, that response should be considered part of the child's repertoire.

In the unstructured observation, the student should be allowed to move freely (or be led) around the music room. Videotape or note responses to social stimuli, motor ability, use of language, problem-solving abilities, and any other behaviors which might be useful in program planning. For example:

- child's reaction to being touched or handled.
- child's awareness of therapist's movements.
- child's response when spoken to pleasantly or given commands.
- child's response to therapist's smile while talking or not.
- child's response to therapist as opposed to those less familiar to him.
- child's self-stimulatory or self-abusive behavior, or any other maladaptive behavior.
- child's length and pitch of vocalizations or verbalizations, as well as number of words used and quality of articulation.
- child's response to sounds in the environment (looks for, searches for, localizes).
- child's cessation of activity when given command "no."
- child's mode of ambulation or locomotion.
- child's length of attention span to people and objects.
- child's use of objects for intended purpose.
- child's ability to generalize from familiar to unfamiliar task or experience.
- child's response to simple direction, such as "give me the _____, please."

This list is not intended to be exhaustive, but to give ideas of things to look for. The information obtained from both the guided and unstructured observations should be put into some structure or form to make it more useful in planning for the child's program.

To summarize considerations for assessment:

1. Assessing is the process of finding out everything pertinent about a child for the purpose of writing meaningful programs.

2. Music therapists are not trained, nor does an adequate tool currently exist, to measure all aspects of a child's behavior.

3. As part of an interdisciplinary team, music therapists should be familiar with the common tests used by other professionals to assess the deaf-blind child, and use these test results to assist in determining appropriate goals for the child.

4. There are many special considerations when assessing the deaf-blind child.

5. Guided observations are useful for determining where the child is functioning and how learning takes place for that particular child.

THE USE OF MUSIC

Very little has been written about music and the deaf-blind child. What is available indicates that rhythm, vibration, and movement are the most important factors when presenting a deaf-blind child with musical experiences. Rhythm is basic to life. Even rhythm that cannot be heard can be felt. In its simplest form, rhythm is experienced in heartbeat, gait, and life cycle. Rhythm also provides persons with energy and order—two very important factors in working with the deaf-blind person.

Music therapy is a discipline through which the majority of multihandicapped children can be served. Cormier (1980) states that:

Music therapy goals incorporate the development, restoration, or alleviation of emotional, physical, and/or intellectual disorders through the sensitive application of music and music activities, e.g., calming music for the distraught or hyperactive child; musical activities which will promote the relaxation and stretching of constricted muscles; and rhythmic activities which may contribute to the development of fine and gross motor skills and, possibly, language development (pp. 26-27).

The role of music in auditory training is emphasized by Cormier (1980), as we read:

Auditory training and discrimination may be enhanced through the use of music, beginning with the fundamental awareness of the presence or absence of sound. Auditory refinement includes: the localization of sound; the source of sound; some characteristics of sound; and the meaning of particular sounds. Vocal sounds used in imitative play strengthens the child's self-awareness as well as proving helpful in establishing communication skills (pp. 33-34).

More than any other discipline, music has the capacity to address itself to the prevailing deficits of the deaf-blind child: limited sensory awareness; lack of sensory integration; minimal environmental awareness of space, objects, and persons.

Before one can meaningfully receive incoming stimuli, there must be an awareness of self, permitting interaction between the stimulating person, object, or event. In other words, one must have a sense of being separate from the stimulus or environment, but aware of its presence and possible effect on our person. "The result of sensory integration dysfunction is a lack of organizing, structuring, and relating of self to objects and objects to objects" (Robinson & Riggio, 1975, p. 3). Sensory integration is a key factor in all learning and is defined as having the ability to receive, interpret, and respond to sensory stimuli. "Sensory input via the sensory systems, combined with memory provide us with perception" (Sage, 1971, p. 72).

Addressing himself to the deaf-blind population in particular, Hammer (1974) defines perception as "the building of sensory inputs and integrating them into patterns of recognition" (p. 18). In this sense, perception becomes meaningful through imitation. The most fundamental aspects of music as found in vibration, rhythm, and movement serve such an imitative purpose. The careful application of these components contribute to the development of self-awareness and of fine and gross motor skills. Rhythm and movement also contribute in the establishment of physical well-being, as well as providing a source of individual or group recreation. To deaf-blind children, music may provide the means of growth in concept development and social skills.

MUSIC AND THE IEP

With the implementation of PL 94-142, deaf-blind children are offered the same educational opportunities as other handicapped children. As any person with a handicapping condition, the deaf-blind child needs special help to achieve educational and developmental potential. Experience has shown that music can be very effective in helping children develop their potential.

Music therapy goals incorporated into the IEP (Individualized Education Program) might include: to provide sensory stimulation, increase self-awareness, develop awareness of others, become aware of the presence or absence of sound, increase attention, and develop awareness of cause and effect. Other goals might be: to increase accuracy in motor responses, and to improve social interaction, sensory integration, and emotional expression. Language and concept development also may be included if the child shows potential for these. It is suggested that these goals be pursued following a developmental sequence when possible. Techniques and goals suggested for music therapy sessions in the section, Developmental Music Guide which follows, are samples of the developmental process. Sensory integration is considered throughout.

Discrimination, communication, and cognition call for meaningful processing ability and, therefore, a functioning level higher than that required for imitation or rote motoric memory. Choice of activities is, then, to be made accordingly. Communication skills and social development are interdependent. Therefore, it is essential to consider the value of nonverbal communication between therapist and child, as conveyed in touch, facial expression, and attitudes.

There is a wide spectrum of skills involved in social development. Some youngsters may not go beyond simple interaction with one adult in a structured setting, while others will benefit from and enjoy peer group activities.

Specific activities listed for the attainment of certain goals may frequently be applied for several purposes, depending on the child's receptivity, age, size, and severity of accompanying handicaps. Goals and activities suggested here in no way exhaust the possibilities. A child's response may create a new idea to which the therapist should respond. It is important to remember that all development in deaf-blind children occurs sporadically. Activities need preparation and introduction in small increments before they can be effective. Splinter skills can be helpful but at times misleading, providing the therapist with mixed results. Awareness of this fact is necessary in the choice of activity and desired goal(s).

The suggested activities are written with a one-therapist, one-child ratio in mind, except for a few group activities where the student number increases. Use of recordings may be eliminated if a therapist has an assistant to provide "live music," leaving the therapist free to interact directly with the child. Experience indicates that all children need some degree of "hands-on" therapy to produce desired results. This can gradually be extinguished, using only occasional prompts (verbal and/or physical) until the child becomes independent (Cormier, 1980).

Praise, affection, and a "favorite activity" have been used to reinforce every effort toward desirable responses. There has been some discussion concerning the use of primary reinforcers as reward. While some music therapists consider them to be valuable, others believe they tend to create uncertainty in cause-and-effect results; these therapists expect the music to be the stimulus and the effective reward. Perhaps judgment on the matter should be left to the professional expertise of the therapist in each case.

CASE STUDY: J

J is a nine-year-old boy who is developmentally delayed, has vision and hearing impairments and many "autistic-like" behaviors. In the past, J was extremely hyperactive and manipulative. Very little progress was being made in social, academic, and behavioral goals.

At the age of seven, J was evaluated by the music therapist. It was observed that J was very involved in self-stimulating and hyperactive behaviors. Although very agile in gross and fine motor movements, all actions were undirected and haphazard. J had no speech nor any other mode of communication. Musically, J indicated interest in and curiosity about the piano and trap set (drums). Other instruments were systematically dropped or tossed in the air.

J was enrolled in the music therapy program for the purpose of decreasing hyperactive behavior and increasing attention span. Music therapy sessions were held four times a week for fifteen minutes each. A large box was used in which the therapist and J could work undistracted by environmental stimuli. Eventually, music sessions were conducted in the room with structure for support against distractions. The electric piano with headset was to be the most effective instrument for the first weeks "out of the box." The very act of playing at the piano provided spatial limitations so needed by J.

Although initially resisting the headset attached to the electric piano, J gradually came to tolerate it enough to add this as a viable goal. This was in preparation for a formal audiological test which was to be conducted at a nearby clinic.

Following several months of very structured music therapy sessions, J progressed to new goals. These were: (1) to improve receptive and expressive language; (2) to improve social behavior; and (3) to refine gross and fine motor skills. Music activities included games requiring interaction between the therapist and J; various instruments and language boards to help in the development of sign language; rhythmic vocal sounds in various pitches to help in the overall gains in social interaction, attention, and language development.

In response to a combination of structure, creativity, patience, and music activities, J made great strides in the areas of academic, behavioral, and social development. After two calendar years, music therapy sessions were considered no longer necessary and J was dismissed from the program.

DEVELOPMENTAL MUSIC GUIDE

Musical Stimulus	Goal(s)	Pre-requisite(s)	Material(s)	Technique—Positioning
vibration	—sensory stimulation —self-awareness	—trust —passive acceptance	triangle bells rhythm sticks cymbals, etc.	a) therapist plays the instrument and holds it against the child's fingers, hands, arms, legs, back, or bare feet, while the instrument is vibrating b) attention is given to child's tolerance and responses c) allow/encourage child to explore the instrument d) place one stick between child's teeth, *gently* tap with other stick
vibration	—sensory stimulation —self-awareness	—size of child must be small enough to fit on top of piano in seated or prone position —trust —passive acceptance	piano	a) place child on the piano in whatever position seems most secure b) therapist plays, observing reactions of the child to various changes in rhythm, pitch, and intensity c) if child is too large to be safely placed on the piano, a wooden platform under the piano or bass drum can be effective
vibration	—sensory stimulation —self-awareness	—trust —passive acceptance	guitar bass xylophone gong mallets	a) therapist plays guitar while child's bare feet or hands rest on the body of the guitar, or fingers rest gently across vibrating strings b) therapist plays xylophone while child's bare feet or hands rest on xylophone stand c) therapist plays gong in various rhythms while child's bare feet are touching edge of gong
vibration	—sensory stimulation —self-awareness	—trust —passive acceptance	snare, bass, or tympani mallets	a) place child's fingers or hand lightly on drum head while therapist plays b) with child lying on the floor, place child's bare feet against drum head while therapist plays
vibration	—sensory stimulation —self-awareness	—trust —passive acceptance —behavioral control	stereo set and speakers recording	a) position same as above while recording is played at a variety of volume, bass, and treble levels while feet or hands on speaker(s)

Musical Stimulus	Goal(s)	Pre-requisite(s)	Materials	Technique— Positioning
vibration	—sensory stimulation —self-awareness	—trust —passive acceptance —behavioral control	double bass	a) position same as above while therapist plucks strings b) place child's back against double bass held in upright position by the therapist c) lay double bass on side with child's back up against it
vibration	—sensory stimulation —self-awareness —awareness of another	—trust —tolerance of physical contact —age/size of child	none	a) hold child on lap while singing to child b) place child's head against singer's chest and/or throat c) place child's hand on singer's throat
vibration rhythm melody	—self-awareness —awareness/other —cause/effect —child vocal response	—tolerance of physical contact	piano	a) therapist seated at piano, plays with one hand and the other on child's throat; child has one hand on therapist's throat
rhythm melody	—awareness/other —child response —interaction —attention span	—tolerance of physical contact	none	a) therapist and child seated opposite each other's shoulders, while therapist taps short, simple rhythm patterns b) as above, add singing by the therapist c) encourage child to make any kind of vocal sounds d) encourage child to imitate rhythm patterns on therapist's shoulders
melody auditory stimulation rhythmic movement	—auditory-motor —appropriate play —attention span —peer interaction —gross-motor coordination —following directions	—behavioral control —simple communication skills, signed or spoken	piano, drum and mallet chairs recording stereo set	a) demonstration of "musical chairs" game by therapist and other staff member, using presence/absence of sound for movement cues b) begin with two children and one chair, all taking turns until game is understood; gradually add number of children and corresponding number of chairs

Musical Stimulus	Goal(s)	Pre-requisite(s)	Material(s)	Technique— Positioning
melody harmony auditory stimula-tion rhythmic movement	—group activity —auditory-motor —gross/fine motor coordination —appropriate play —peer interaction —following	—behavioral control —sufficient hearing —sufficient motor control —simple communi-cation skills, signed or spoken	1 hula hoop per couple recording: *Wake Up, Calm Down* Elizabeth Polk, Educational Activities, Inc. AR 695	1) follow instructions on record jacket of *Wake Up, Calm Down* by Elizabeth Polk for selection Shoe-maker's Dance " Wind the Bobbin" b) demonstrate step-by-step, allowing practice time on individual basis c) encourage child to join game a little at a time
melody auditory stimula-tion rhythmic movement	—peer interaction —following directions —group activity —development of visual-motor skill	—mobility —potential for following	recording: *I'm Not Small* Zeitlin-Berman, Educational Activities, Inc. AR 547	a) step-by-step explanation and demonstration by therapist and two children b) follow instructions in book-let accompanying record-ing of *I'm Not Small* Zeitlin-Berman, for selection "Dance Around" c) encourage child to join in game a little at a time

FACILITATION OF ACTIVITIES

Because music has an effect on human physiology (Eagle, 1978; Hodges, 1980), it is necessary to be informed of the child's neurological condition, especially in the case of seizure activity and/or severe spasticity. In such instances, it is recommended that the musical stimulus be considered carefully, using that which reflects predictable rhythms, medium pitch, and nonabrasive instrumental qualities. Although instrumental sounds are not intrinsically abrasive, particular sounds may be irritating or aversive to individual persons and certain neurological conditions. With a spastic child, it is more effective to begin rhythm/motor development by utilizing the child's own natural body rhythm before attempting to impose another. The reason for this is three-fold: 1) it is developmentally sound to begin with assets the child already has, 2) it promotes relaxation of muscles, and 3) it promotes success and positive feedback for the child (Cormier, 1980, pp. 39-40).

Although it is desirable to use large floor space, children who exhibit poor attention and/or hyperactive behavior usually benefit from limited space at first, e.g., a chair, mat, hulahoop, or large box. Locomotor activities should begin "in place" to help the child establish organization of the desired rhythmic pattern, giving the hyperactive child a sense of direction. These precautions permit gradual gain in confidence and self-control while keeping disciplinary measures at a minimum.

When a blind child is about to be introduced to unusually loud sounding instruments, it is important to allow preliminary tactile and auditory exploration of the instrument. Deaf-blind children also learn from oral exploration. This is to be permitted whenever it is safe to do so. This type of exploration is a good developmental technique and minimizes the possiblity of negative neurological, behavioral, and emotional effects triggered by surprise.

If the use of recordings is desirable or necessary, the following points are to be considered.

1. Volume/loudness should be monitored carefully, especially if the child is wearing hearing aids; hearing deficits are often related to pitch or quality of sound. Loud volume is sometimes painful and detrimental to the child.

2. Instrumental renditions are most effective; deaf-blind children cannot discriminate recorded lyrics nor can they process these rapidly enough, if at all.

3. If a child appears to respond to low pitches, increase bass and decrease treble on stereo component; do the opposite if the child responds better to high pitches.

4. Musical selections of definite, clear rhythmic accent are most effective.

5. A stereo system is preferred to a monaural set.

INTERDISCIPLINARY TEAMS AND MUSIC THERAPY

The versatility of music as an educational, developmental, or remedial medium is compatible with goals stated by teachers, speech therapists, occupational therapists, and physical therapists. Music activities can also play a major role in the development of the child's sense of self and body-image. These music activities may correlate with goals stated by a recreation therapist.

A speech therapist and music therapist may collaborate in the planning and implementation of a language program for a child, beginning with babbling sounds, development of rhythm patterns, auditory discrimination, sequential memory patterns, and particular word sounds and blends commonly found in songs. Melodic patterns help to enhance vocal inflection when speech is a realistic goal for a particular child. Should sign language be the most appropriate mode of communication for the child, the rhythmic musical experience can help ease the flow of manual signing.

Occupational therapists and music therapists provide complementary activities in the area of gross motor, visual-motor, and locomotor coordination. Music's influence on physiological responses calls for communication between music and physical therapists as well as with occupational therapists. A child who needs physical relaxation and stretching or one whose needs are in the area of stimulation can easily be served by the appropriate choice of music for listening, or music which demands active, physical response. These music sessions, planned in conjunction with physical and occupational therapists, will be all the more beneficial to the child.

Last, but not least, we consider music as an educational medium. This is evident when one reflects on the many ways in which musical experiences might present or reinforce number concepts, shapes, colors, phrasing, and so forth. Many music activities planned by the music therapist, in conjunction with IEP goals, may be carried out or reinforced by the teaching staff. Teachers are also valuable resources for pertinent information about the children, which might prove helpful to the therapist.

The developing child will be all the richer if the adults in the child's life make a concerted effort to work together, supporting the parents of the child as well as each other, in the dream of helping the multihandicapped child become as ready as possible to reach whatever potential is meant to be.

REFERENCE NOTES

1. Major portions of this section were contributed by Sara A. Carter, RMT, Sunland Training Center, Tallahassee, Florida.

2. Annotated bibliography contributed by Juanita McIlwaine, RMT, Eastern New Mexico University, Portales.

REFERENCES

Cormier, L. *A guide in the use of music in the training and development of rubella deaf-blind children.* Unpublished master's thesis, Michigan State University, East Lansing, 1980.

Dantona, R. A history of centers and services for deaf-blind children. *State of the Art—Perspectives on Serving Deaf-Blind Children.* Sacramento: California State Department of Education, 1974.

Dantona, R. Centers and services for deaf-blind children: past, present, and future. *Selected Papers, Fifty-Third Biennial Conferences.* Philadelphia: Association for the Education of the Visually Handicapped, 1976.

Diebold, M. H., Curtis, M. C. & Dubose, R. F. Developmental scales versus observational measures for deaf-blind children. *Exceptional Children*, 1978, *44*, 175-278.

Eagle, C. T., Jr. (Ed.) *Music therapy index, Volume 1.* Lawrence, KS: National Association for Music Therapy, 1976.

Eagle, C. T., Jr. (Ed.) *Music psychology index, Volume 2.* Denton, TX: National Institute for Therapeutics Research, 1978.

Hammer, E. K. *Psychological assessment of the deaf-blind child: The synthesis of assessment and educational services.* Paper presented at the International Seminar on Deaf-Blind, Royal Institute for the Blind, Condover, Shrewsbury, England, 1974.

Hodges, D. A. Physiological responses to music. In D. A. Hodges (Ed.), *Handbook of music psychology.* Lawrence, KS: National Association for Music Therapy, 1980.

Holm, V. Multiple handicaps: A developmental approach to their assessment. *Proceedings Workshop for Serving the Deaf-Blind and Multihandicapped Child: Identification, Assessment, and Training.* Sacramento: California State Department of Education, 1979.

Robinson, C. & Riggio, M. *Jean Ayres' sensory integrative approach.* Dallas: Callier Center for Communication Disorders, 1975.

Sage, G. H. *Introduction to motor behavior: A neuropsychological approach.* Reading, MA: Addison-Wesley, 1971.

Wabash Center for the Mentally Retarded. *Guide to early developmental training.* Boston: Allyn and Bacon, 1977.

Waterhouse, E. J. Education of the deaf-blind in the United States of America, 1837-1967. *State of the Art—Perspectives on Serving Deaf-Blind Children.* Sacramento: California State Department of Education, 1977.

ANNOTATED BIBLIOGRAPHY[2]

Anderson, C. *Teaching deaf-blind children with materials found in the home.* Nashville: George Peabody College, Child Study Center.

Materials listed are commonly found in homes. Details on how to use materials to meet objective goals are given.

Ficociello, C. & Rudin, D. *Moovin' and groovin': A program for the development of auditory-motor integration.* Dallas: South Central Regional Center, 1975.

This program is contained on a set of cards arranged developmentally. For each activity, the following is included: objective, rationale, materials, method, and modifications. Many of the activities are musically oriented.

Granberry, G. L. *Fine motor skills for the classroom.* Ellisville, Mississippi: Ellisville State School Residential Deaf-Blind Program.

Contains lists which are useful for reference, such as a list of sequential developmental steps, a list of definitions of motor terms, and suggested sequential fine motor skills.

Hedrick, D.L. et al. *Communicator programs for the multi-handicapped deaf-blind child.* Seattle: Northwest Regional Center for Services to Deaf-Blind Children.

A complete communication program, which is based on a developmental model. It begins on a low level.

Kentucky School for the Blind. *Program planning, implementation, and evaluation for deaf-blind children,* 1977.

An excellent resource book. Included are an evaluation, examples of IEPs, individual planning cards, lists of developmental motor charts. Objectives and procedures are given for specific areas. Programs for specific senses include the near senses.

Meshcheriakov, A. I. The main principles of the system for education and training of the blind and deaf and dumb. *The Education of the Blind,* December, 1962, 43-48.

This Russian author deals with the first stages of development of deaf-blind. Emphasis is placed on "initial humanizing."

Mikalonis, L. et al. *Leisure time activities for deaf-blind children.* Joyce Motion Picture Company, 1974.

Many activities are listed which could be used for learning experiences as well as leisure-time activities. For each activity, the following is included: purposes, materials, procedures, picture illustrations, observed behaviors, desired behaviors, and cautions. A realistic approach is used.

Peabody College for Teachers. *A beginning motor program for multiple handicapped children.* Nashville: Peabody College for Teachers, 1971.

Sections include body-image, balance, position in space, locomotion, eye-hand coordination, eye-foot coordination, muscle strength, and eurythmics. Stick drawings illustrate activities.

Peabody College for Teachers. *Recipes for homemade materials and activities for deaf-blind children.* Nashville: Peabody College for Teachers.

Materials which are easily found are listed and directions are given for use.

Russo, R. & Wousburger, B. H. *Exercises for deaf-blind children.* Talledega, Alabama: Southeast Regional Center for Deaf-Blind Children.

Detailed exercise routines are given which are designed to improve large muscle groups of the body and to insure necessary range of motion in all joints so normal posture and gait can be attained.

Texas Education Agency. *Educational methods for deaf-blind and severely handicapped students* (Vols. I, II) Austin: Texas Education Agency, 1979.

This is a good source for information about equipment which is available, including pictures, descriptions, and prices.

SELECTED READINGS AND RESOURCES

California State Department of Education. *Literature on deaf blind: An annotated bibliography.* Sacramento: California State Department of Education, 1976.

Clark, C. & Chadwick, D. *Clinically adapted instruments for the multiply handicapped.* Westford, Massachusetts: Modulations Company, 1979.

Fukurai, S. *How can I make what I cannot see?* New York: Van Nostrand Reinhold, 1974.

Hammer, E. K. *Deaf-blind children: A list of references.* Dallas: Callier Hearing and Speech Center, n.d.

Meyer, S. & Thielman, V. *John Tracy Clinic correspondence learning program for parents of preschool deaf/blind children.* Los Angeles: John Tracy Clinic, n.d.

Purvis, J. & Samet, S. (Eds.). *Music in developmental therapy: A curriculum guide.* Baltimore: University Park Press, 1976.

White, A. *Performing toys.* New York: Taplinger Publishing, 1970.

Zimmerman, M. *Musical characteristics of children.* Reston, VA: Music Educators' National Conference, 1971.

SELECTED ASSESSMENT INSTRUMENTS

Assessment of auditory functioning of deaf-blind multihandicapped children, by D. Kukla & T. Thomas. Dallas: South Central Regional Center for Services to Deaf-Blind Children.

Bayley scales of infant development behavior test. New York: The Psychological Corporation.

Callier-Azusa scale, by R. Stillman (Ed.). Dallas: Callier Center for Communication Disorders.

Deaf-blind program and ability screening test, by Lyall, Henry, Graham & Lassiter. Ellisville, Mississippi: Deaf-Blind Evaluation Center.

Denver developmental screening test, by W. K. Frakenburg & J. B. Dodds. Denver: University of Colorado Medical School.

Developmental activities screening inventory, by R. Dubose. Boston: Teaching Resources.

Hiskey-Nebraska test of learning aptitude, by M. S. Hiskey. Lincoln: Author.

Learning accomplishment profile, by A. Sanford. Winston-Salem: Kaplan Press.

Learning accomplishment profile for infants, by A. Sanford. Winston-Salem: Kaplan Press.

The Leiter international performance scale, by R. G. Leiter. Chicago: Stoelting Company.

Uzgiris-Hunt ordinal scales of psychological development. Urbana: University of Illinois.

Vineland social maturity scale, by E. A. Doll. Minneapolis: American Guidance Services.

SELECTED FILMS

The Deaf-Blind Child, 16mm sound/color, 23 min; Title #260410; from the European Series: International Education of the Hearing Impaired Child. Rent or purchase from National Audiovisual Center, General Services Administration, Washington, DC 20409.

Sensory Stimulation #2: Beginning Communication, 20 min. Rent free from South Central Regional Center for Services to Deaf-Blind Children, Callier Center for Communication Disorders, Dallas, Texas 75235.

Sensory Stimulation #4: Tactile, 20 min. Rent free from South Central Regional Center for Services to Deaf-Blind Children, Callier Center for Communication Disorders, Dallas, Texas 75235.

Sensory Stimulation #5: Auditory, 20 min. Rent free from South Central Regional Center for Services to Deaf-Blind Children, Callier Center for Communication Disorders, Dallas, Texas 75235.

SELECTED RECORDINGS

Resources

Children's Book and Music Center
2500 Santa Monica Boulevard
Santa Monica, CA 90404

Educational Activities, Inc.
P.O. Box 392
Freeport, Long Island, NY 11520

Kimbo Educational
10-16 North Third Avenue
P.O. Box 477
Long Branch, NJ 07740

Lyons
530 Riverview Avenue
Elkhart, IN 46514

From Children's Book and Music Center:

Adventures in Music. Complete 12-record set—M654
RCA Recordings, Gladys Tipton, Editor

Dance Music for Pre-School Children—PE148
Bruce King, Douglas Nordli

Lullabies from Around the World—M906
Marilyn Horne, Richard Robinson

More Learning as We Play—SE228
Winifred Stiles, David Ginglend

Pictures At An Exhibition—M633
Modeste Moussorgsky

From Educational Activities, Inc.:

"I'm Not Small—AR547
"Dance Around" circle game
Patty Zeitlin, Marcia Berman

Mod Marches—AR527
Hap Palmer

Modern Tunes for Rhythms and Instruments—AR523
Hap Palmer

Movin'—AR546
Hap Palmer

Rhythms for Today—HYP29
Carrie Rasmussen, Violet Stewart

The Feel of Music—AR556
Hap Palmer

Wake Up! Calm Down! Volume 1—AR659
Elizabeth Polk

From Kimbo Educational:

Music for Movement Exploration—LP5090
Karol Lee

Pretend—EA563
(instrumental side)
Hap Palmer

Sea Gulls—EA584
Hap Palmer

SUPPORT ORGANIZATIONS

Regional Centers for Services to Deaf-Blind Children

Centers and Services for Deaf-Blind
Children
Office of Special Education
Donohoe Building
7th and D Streets, S.W.
Washington, DC 20202

Mid-Atlantic (North) and Carribean
Regional Center and Services to
Deaf-Blind Children
999 Pelham Parkway
Bronx, NY 10469

Mid-West Regional Center and Services
to Deaf-Blind Children
P.O. Box 420
Lansing, MI 48902

Mountain Plains Regional Center for
Services to Deaf-Blind Children
165 Cook Street, Suite 304
Denver, CO 80206

New England Regional Center for
Services to Deaf-Blind Children
175 North Beacon Street
Watertown, MA 02172

Northwest Regional Center for Services
to Deaf-Blind Children
3411 South Alaska Street
Seattle, WA 98118

South Atlantic Regional Center for
Services to Deaf-Blind Children
Educational Building, Room 449
Edenton and Salisbury Streets
Raleigh, NC 27611

South Central Regional Center for
Services to Deaf-Blind Children
Callier Center for Communication Disorders
1966 Inwood Road
Dallas, TX 75235

Southeast Regional Center for Deaf-Blind
Children
P.O. Box 698
Talladega, AL 35160

Southwestern Regional Deaf-Blind Center
721 Capitol Mall
Sacramento, CA 95814

Texas Regional Center for Services to
Deaf-Blind Children
Texas Education Agency
201 East 11th Street
Austin, TX 78701

Other Agencies and Organizations Serving Deaf-Blind Persons

Helen Keller National Center for
Deaf-Blind Youths and Adults
111 Middle Neck Road
Sands Point, NY 11050

ERIC Documents
Bethesda, MD
(especially ERIC nos. ED 040-520 and ED 005-373)

Library of Congress
Division for the Blind and Physically Handicapped,
 or Music Division
1291 Taylor Street
Washington, DC 20542

Sigma Alpha Iota
International Music Fraternity
268 Shore Drive East
Bay Heights
Miami, FL 33133
(Large print source)